THE SPANISH

Members of the Republican semi-Trotskyist Marxist Poum Militia, display a show of force at the Karl Marx barracks in Barcelona.

I urged Hitler to give support under all circumstances, firstly in order to prevent the further spread of Communism in that theatre and, secondly, to test my young Luftwaffe at this opportunity in this or that technical respect.

"With the permission of the Führer, I sent a large part of my transport fleet and a number of experimental fighter units, bombers and anti-aircraft guns; and in that way I had the opportunity to ascertain, under combat conditions, whether the material was equal to the task. In order that the personnel, too, might gather a certain amount of experience, I saw to it that there was a continuous flow, that is, that new people were constantly being sent and others recalled.

Hermann Göring at the Nuremberg War Trials

March 1946

The Background

In order to understand why Germany became involved in the Spanish Civil War, it is necessary to describe the political background that led to its origin. By the early 1900s, Spain was divided into two mutually hostile social groups, with landowners and industrialists on one side and landless labourers and peasants on the other. The advance of Socialism and anarchism among urban workers led the more far-sighted landowners to try and stop this spreading to the countryside. Counter-revolutionary syndicates were financed by landlords from 1906 and in 1912 a group of dynamic social Catholics led by Angel Herrera helped establish a series of powerful Agrarian Federations. These Right-Wing organisations tried to improve the lives of impoverished farmers by offering them credit facilities, agricultural expertise, warehousing and machinery in return for their adoption of virulent anti-socialism. Nevertheless Left Wing urban unrest continued, so much so that the army was forced to crush the striking Socialists in August 1917 in a bloody operation. The Right Wing industrialists were still fearful of militant workers on the streets however, and this forced them to drop their own political demands and join in a coalition government in 1918 with the Liberals and Conservatives.

The defeat of the urban Socialists in 1917 did not, however, mark the end of the attack on the Right Wing. Between 1918 and 1921, anarchist labourers from the south took part in a series of uprisings which, although crushed again by the army and civil guard, intensified social resentment in the rural south. The end of the First World War had also resulted in the revival of foreign trade competition and the consequent European recession also hit Spain. To counter this, the Catalonian industrialists in particular, introduced a series of wage cuts and lay offs which resulted in a spiralling of urban violence, particularly in Barcelona.

On 23 September 1923, the Right Wing General, Miguel Primo de Rivera, Captain-General of Barcelona, carried out a *coup d'état* after having accused the parliamentary government of leading the country to ruin. King Alfonso XIII then entrusted the government to Primo de Rivera who, though arbitrary, was a dictator of some mildness and charm and outwardly restored order. A brief golden age began. The calm was superficial and discontent increased. In January 1930, the King abruptly withdrew his support from Primo de Rivera. Alfonso then tried to return to the system of alternative moderate Liberal and Conservative governments, but these were unable to control the upsurge of Left Wing Republicanism. In the municipal elections of April 1931 the Republicans won an overwhelming majority and Alfonso bowed to the result and left Spain.

Alcalá Zamora, an Andalusian, then became first prime minister of a moderate but weak provisional government which was incapable of maintaining order. Riots broke out all over Spain during which churches and convents were burned and looted. In June 1931, a constituent parliament was elected and the success of the Republican coalition was confirmed by the voters. Zamora was appointed president of Spain in December 1931, trying in vain to steer a middle course between the Left and Right.

For the following two years the country was governed by the Socialist Majority led by the Leftist writer and intellectual, Manuel Azaña. In August 1932, General José Sanjurjo led a Right Wing military insurrection against this government, but it was crushed without difficulty. Elections were then held in November 1933 which resulted in the victory of the CEDA or Catholic Party led by José Maria Gil Robles. Relying on the support of various Right Wing groups, the party was to trigger a revolution in October 1934 when Catalan Nationalists, Socialists and Asturian miners rose against it, giving a foretaste of what was to come. The revolution was brutally suppressed and Azaña imprisoned.

On 18 February 1936, hoping that a centre party would at last emerge between the warring political extremes, President Zamora called an election, but the Left Wing or Popular Front gained control of the country and Anzaña again became prime minister. The situation rapidly deteriorated. The state was powerless to deal with the violence of various antagonistic elements and had proved incapable of carrying out the necessary reforms. On 13 July 1936, a former Conservative minister and now effectively leader of the Right Wing opposition, José Calvo Sotelo, was murdered two days after he was openly threatened by a Communist deputy. Four days later, a military uprising began, ostensibly with the aim of restoring order.

The first leader of the military backlash was General Emilio Mola and it was planned to make Sanjurjo – the leader of the earlier failed coup – the figurehead. Another of the conspirators was General Francisco Franco, who had earlier been relieved of his post as Chief of General Staff by the Republicans and made Governor of the Canary Islands. As the revolution developed, Franco was flown from the Canary Islands to Spanish Morocco which had already fallen to the Nationalists and where some 47,000 well-trained troops were based. On 19 July, Sanjurjo was killed when his aircraft crashed on take-off from Portugal, and this and other factors led to Franco, who outranked Mola, becoming the preferred leader of the rebellion. By 22 July 1936, Spain was divided, with the Leftist Republicans in control of much of the south and east, plus a northern coastal strip including Oviedo, Santander and Bilbao, whilst the Nationalists held the remainder of the country plus the cities of Sevilla and Cadiz in the south. (See map on page 100).

Germany becomes involved

The events outlined in "The Background" on page 2 presented General Franco with the problem of transporting his troops, in particular a large number of Moorish soldiers, to the mainland to support the uprising. On 22 July, he made an urgent appeal, via the offices of Adolf Langenheim, head of the Nazi Party in Tetuán, and Johannes Bernhardt, a German businessman in Morocco, to Hitler. The *Führer*, who had just returned from attending a performance of the opera *Die Walküre* in Bayreuth, was initially cool about supporting the revolt, but after haranguing his audience about the evils of Bolshevism, he became a shrewd supporter. Still under the influence of the "Magic Fire" music which accompanies Siegfried's passage through the flames to rescue Brünnhilde, he decided to call the German involvement *Unternehmen Feuerzauber* (Operation Magic Fire).

Hitler's first act was to establish COS 'W', a department in the German War Ministry intended to co-ordinate the recruitment of "volunteers" and the dispatch of war material to Spain. Two holding companies were then formed through which all materials for Spain would be handled. These were HISMA *(Compañiá Hispano Marroquí de Transportes)* and ROWAK *(Rohstoffe und Waren Einkaufgesellschaft)*. Any material intended for the Spanish Nationalists would first be sold to ROWAK, with HISMA marketing them in Spain.

General Francisco Franco Bahamonde was born in 1892 and rose to become army Chief of General Staff. The Republicans relieved him of this post shortly before the outbreak of the Spanish Civil War and made him Governor of the Canary Islands. As the revolution developed, Franco was chosen to lead all Nationalist forces. After the successful conclusion of the conflict, he dissolved all political parties except the Falange and began a period of authoritarian rule which probably did much to modernise Spain. He eventually restored the monarchy, acting as regent until his death in 1975 when he was succeeded by King Juan Carlos.

The first aircraft to be sent to the aid of Franco were 30 Ju 52/3ms which were flown to Morocco. Between 29 July and 5 August, these aircraft flew 1,500 men from Morocco to Sevilla, and in all 10,500 men were transferred to Spain from North Africa in July and August 1936 followed by 9,700 in September. In 1942 Hitler said "Franco ought to erect a monument to the glory of the Junkers 52."

At the same time as the supply of the Ju 52/3ms, *Oberst* Alexander von Scheele established the *Reisegesellschaft* – "Tourist Company" – which was to transport volunteers to Spain to help man Nationalist Army units. The first combat aircraft to leave Germany were six Heinkel He 51 fighters which were shipped on the *Usaramo* from Hamburg on 1 August 1936 together with 86 men. These included ten transport crews and six fighter pilots: Kraft Eberhardt, Herwig Knüppel, Hannes Trautloft, Wolf-Heinrich von Houwald, Ekkehard Hefter and Gerhard Klein. The pilots were told to avoid combat, their main task being to protect the Ju 52/3ms ferrying troops from Tetuán to Sevilla.

Spanish Nationalist troops preparing to board Ju 52/3ms early in the Civil War. Because the Spanish Navy had remained largely Republican, it was impossible for Franco to ferry his experienced Moorish troops from Morocco to Spain by sea. The solution came in the form of twenty Ju 52 and eleven SM.81 transport aircraft donated by Germany and Italy respectively.

July to October 1936

Generalleutnant Helmuth Wilberg, a First World War pilot who was appointed head of the Special Headquarters for German-Spanish Military Aid. Prior to his appointment, Wilberg had been commander of a Luftkreisschule.

In July 1936, Oberst Alexander von Scheele established the Reisegesellschaft which co-ordinated the transport of German volunteers to Spain.

With the support of the German government Josef Veltjens, an arms dealer, supplied much of the early war material sent to Spain. During the First World War, Veltjens had served as a fighter pilot with Jasta 18 and JG 2, claiming 34 victories and being awarded the Pour le Mérite.

The first six German fighter pilots sent to Spain still in their civilian clothes. From left are: Lt. Gerhard Klein (shot down and killed by flak on 18 January 1938 on the Teruel front), Lt. Ekkehard Hefter (killed in an accident on 28 September 1936 due to engine failure at Vitoria, the first fighter pilot to be killed in Spain), Oblt. Hannes Trautloft, Oblt. Herwig Knüppel, Oblt. Kraft Eberhardt (killed in combat on 13 November 1936 at Casa de Campo) and Lt. Wolf-Heinrich von Houwald.

Following the *Usaramo's* arrival at Cadiz on 7 August, the fighter pilots took a train to Sevilla-Tablada airfield where they were joined by a number of engineers and technicians. Assembly of the He 51s commenced on 11 August and for a short period these were flown by a group of five Spanish pilots. On 18 August, *Capt.* Garcia Morato shot down a Potez 540 bomber, but one of the He 51s was seriously damaged in a landing accident. On 22 August, the five remaining Heinkels flew to Escalona del Prado airfield via Salamanca to support General Mola's advance on Madrid. Next day, eight Ju 52/3ms and three He 51s raided Getafe airfield near Madrid, but the Spanish pilots managed to crash two more Heinkels on landing. Following this, Scheele pleaded that the German pilots be allowed to fly combat missions and, on 25 August, the first aerial victories were claimed by the German pilots when *Oberleutnante* Eberhardt and Trautloft both shot down a Breguet XIX. Next day, two more Breguet XIXs were claimed followed by a Nieuport 52 on the 27th and a Potez 540 on the 29th. On 30 August, three more Potez 540s were destroyed but Trautloft's He 51 was shot down. He survived unscathed.

During September, more He 51s and pilots arrived in Spain, some of the survivors of the first batch being passed to the Spaniards. The arrival of the new aircraft allowed a second He 51 *Kette* to be established at Caceres under von Houwald. On 23 September, the He 51 units were transferred to Vitoria to support the Nationalist advance towards the northern coast. Five days later, one of the new arrivals, *Lt.* Hefter was killed when the wing of his He 51 struck the tower of the town hall at Vitoria during the transfer from there to Ávila.

By the end of September, ten more pilots had arrived in Spain: von Bothmer, von Gilsa, Gödecke, Kowalski, Henrici, Mratzek, Radusch, Rehahn, Sawallisch and Strümpell. In mid October a number of He 51s were transferred to the Aragon area to act as protection for the Spanish piloted He 46s. The first action came on 19 October when 13 Republican aircraft attacked the Heinkels, but lost five of their number, three to *Lt.* Oskar Henrici.

On 8 November, the Nationalists launched a drive on Madrid and the Republican militia fought desperately to defend the capital. Around this time the first Soviet Polikarpov I-15 and I-16 fighters had begun to arrive in Spain and on 11 November, a Republican air raid on Ávila destroyed several He 46s, He 51s and Ju 52/3ms. Two days later, the remaining He 51s, in company with a squadron of Fiat C.R.32s, clashed with I-15s for the first time; Eberhardt, the commander of the German *Staffel,* and Henrici were killed. By 15 November, the *Staffel*, now commanded by Knüppel, only had three He 51s on strength.

RIGHT: On 23 August 1936, two of the six He 51s which arrived in Spain suffered crash landings at the hands of Spanish pilots. This aircraft is unusual in that it only has the number "5" painted on the fuselage side, possibly because the aircraft type code "2" had not then been allocated.

BELOW: One of the first of six He 51s to arrive in Spain, coded 2●2. At this time, the aircraft had overall pale grey finish with simple black and white national insignia and black numbers. The aircraft in the background is a Fokker F VII/3 three-engined transport.

Heinkel He 51 B-1

An aircraft of the first volunteer unit sent to Spain, August 1936. This machine was damaged on landing at Escalona airfield on 23 August whilst in the hands of a Spanish pilot. At this stage, the aircraft type code had not been painted on the fuselage. Later a number "2" for the He 51 was applied in front of the black national insignia circle, the number "1" having been allocated to the Nieuport 52.

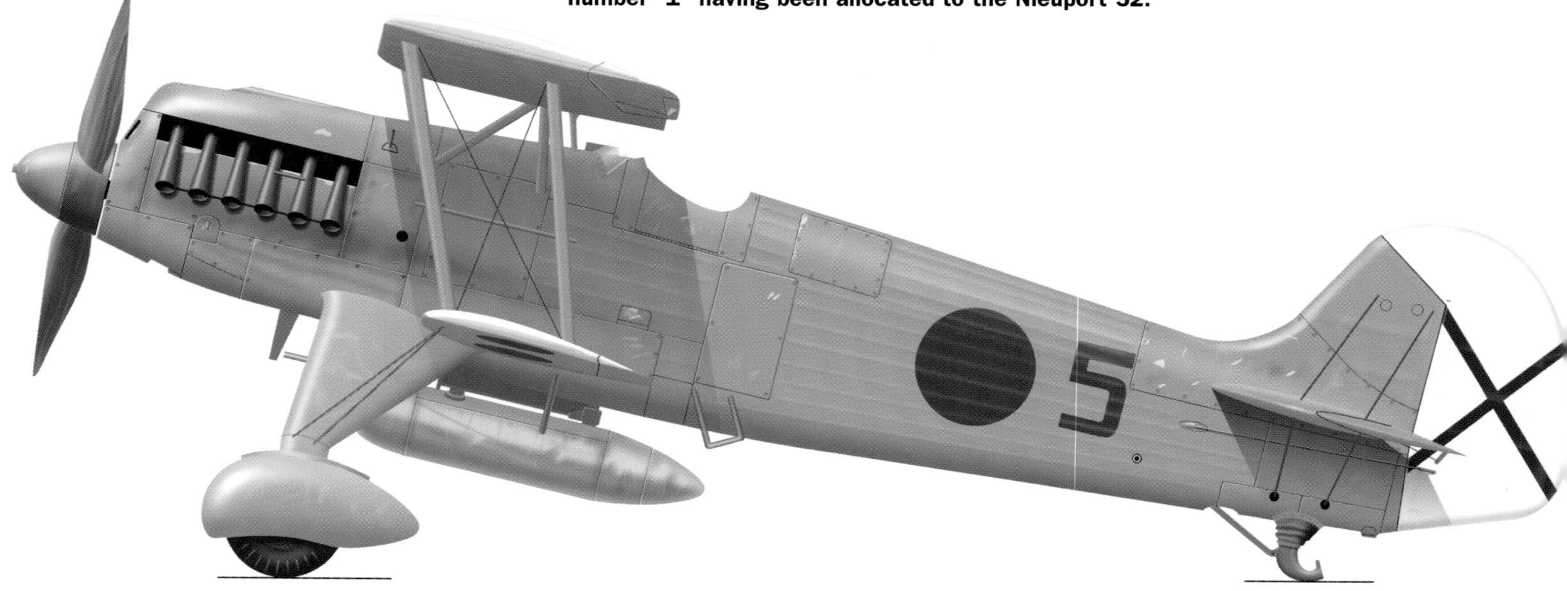

We waited in sports clothing for our first operational mission...

HANNES TRAUTLOFT

Hannes Trautloft was one of the *Luftwaffe's* most capable fighter commanders not only in terms of his number of victories, but for his command abilities. He was *Geschwaderkommodore* of JG 54 *"Grünherz"* from August 1940 until July 1943 before going on to serve in various staff and command positions, including a period as *Inspekteur der Tagjäger* - Inspector for Day Fighters. An intelligent, outspoken man, he was never afraid to criticise the way he saw Göring leading the *Luftwaffe* to ruin and his comments and opinions made him unpopular with various influential factions within the senior command of the *Luftwaffe*. Trautloft, awarded the *Ritterkreuz* on 27 July 1941, flew 560 operational missions and is accredited with 58 confirmed victories, five of which were scored during the Spanish Civil War. He died in 1995.

"On 1 April 1932, I entered the *Deutsche Verkehrfliegerschule* - German Air Transport School - in Schleissheim and after about eight months there, had the opportunity to be sent to Lipezk in the Soviet Union for "secret" training. When I returned to Germany some four months later, I volunteered for service in the Army and was quite naturally posted to the *Luftwaffe* once Hitler embarked on rebuilding Germany's armed forces.

"In 1934, I was back in Schleissheim, but this time as a *Leutnant*, at the *Jagdfliegerschule*. On 28 July 1936, whilst I was serving as an *Oberleutnant* with 9./JG 134 at Köln, I received a telephone call from my *Kommandeur, Hptm*. Oskar Dinort. His first question was: *"Are you engaged to be married?"* I stated that I was not. He then swore me to secrecy and began to explain to me about the situation in Spain and the need for well trained pilots in that country.

"Before he even had the chance to ask me if I would be prepared to go there, I said to him: *"I volunteer!"*

"Dinort then told me to get ready to travel to Dortmund within the next two hours where I would receive orders directly from a *Geschwaderkommodore*. He also ordered me to maintain absolute discretion about the whole thing, for it would not be easy to explain to my comrades what I was doing when they saw me hurriedly packing my bags! Upon arrival in Dortmund, towards the end of the day, I met my *Kommodore, Oberst* von Döring. Next day, I journeyed to Berlin where I met about 80 fellow servicemen, including some fighter pilots, with whom I would travel to Spain. We had to hand in our uniforms and as of that day, we were all officially discharged from the armed forces!

"On 1 August, we left Berlin by bus and drove to Hamburg where we embarked on the transport ship *Usaramo*. We helped in the loading of a quantity of large crates in which, I would quickly learn, our aircraft were stowed in disassembled components.

"We all enjoyed the voyage to Spain and on 7 August, we arrived in Cadiz, from where we took a train to Sevilla.

"The next morning, we found ourselves at Sevilla airfield, a frequent target for "Red" airmen. As early as 9 August, we started the job of rebuilding our six He 51s - a real piece of teamwork involving pilots and ground personnel. The Spanish personnel were quite surprised to witness us work with such energy, but we really were getting quite impatient and wanted to get our machines into the air as soon as possible.

"On 11 August, the first He 51 took off with *"Oberleutnant"* (in reality, we were civilians) Kraft Eberhardt at the controls. During the afternoon, I took off in the second one. The next day, during the morning, our third aircraft took off as well (this time piloted by Herwig Knüppel). We felt very proud of our aircraft and waited for the "Reds" ready for combat, despite the fact that we were still civilians and thus without uniforms. The day was very hot and we waited in sports clothing for our first operational mission.

"On 25 August 1936, my friend Eberhardt and I claimed the first German aerial victories in Spain - two Breguet XIXs. I sat in my aircraft in shorts and a T-shirt - my tennis clothes! The next day, our unit claimed two more Breguet XIXs. On the 27th and 29th we had one claim and on 30 August, we shot down three Potez 540s (one of which was my second "kill"). But in spite of these encouraging results, it was clear that our aircraft were not superior enough for us to feel completely safe from the enemy. In fact, on 30 August, I was, for my part, shot down and had to bail out. I was lucky that I was not wounded and that I landed behind Nationalist lines. However, Franco's troops were, of course, not only surprised to see a tennis player landing in their positions by parachute, they were also very suspicious of me. I did not speak Spanish very well and I suppose they thought that I could have been a foreign volunteer for the "Red Army". I proved to them that this was not the case by showing them my passport. In it was written: *"Este aparate y su piloti Don. Hannes Trautloft, estan al servicio del Ejercito Nacional del Norte."*

"After having carefully read these lines, the Spanish officer shook my hand and I was treated in a very friendly fashion.

"In total, I made five claims whilst in Spain; the other three were: a Nieuport 52 on 1 September 1936, a Potez on 30 September and a Rata on 8 December.

"I returned to Germany on 1 March 1937 and very soon began to write my first book, thanks to my private war diary. It would be published in 1939 under the title *As a Fighter Pilot in Spain* and Ernst Udet wrote the introduction."

July to October 1936

ABOVE: Another of the first batch of six He 51s. This was the aircraft in which Oblt. Hannes Trautloft was shot down on 30 August 1936 but managed to bail out safely. This photo, taken at Escalona airfield, shows a Fokker F VII/3 three-engined transport in the background.

Heinkel He 51 B-1

At Escalona airfield, August 1936. This is the aircraft in which Oblt. Hannes Trautloft was shot down on 30 August 1936 becoming the first German fighter to fall victim to a Republican aircraft. Trautloft managed to escape unhurt. The aircraft was finished in overall pale grey (63).

RIGHT: During July and August 1936 fifteen He 51 Bs were delivered to Spain, with another batch of eighteen (including this one) arriving the following month. Eighteen more Heinkels arrived in October with a further twenty-four following in November.

NOVEMBER 1936 TO MARCH 1937

The Legion Condor is formed

Up until the end of October 1936, all German aid to Spain had been given under conditions of strictest secrecy. The pilots who had gone to the country were officially discharged from the German armed forces and wore civilian clothes. The arrival of the first Soviet aircraft, flown by Soviet aircrews as well as the increasing use of "International Brigades" led Germany to rethink its policy. On 7 November, the Legion Condor was established with 4,500 volunteers under the command of *Generalmajor* Hugo Sperrle, with *Oberst* Wolfram *Freiherr* von Richthofen as Chief of Staff. Eventually, the *Luftwaffe* component of the Legion Condor was to reach the size of a *Fliegerkorps* and consisted of the following:

Born in 1895, Generalmajor Hugo Sperrle (code named "Sander" in Spain) served with the German Flying Service during the First World War. He was appointed first commander of the Legion Condor but proved somewhat of an abrasive character. After he returned to Germany in October 1937, he assumed command of Luftwaffengruppen-kommando *3* (later Luftflotte *3*). In August 1944, at the age of 59, he was transferred to the reserve.

A/88	Reconnaissance *Gruppe* with two *Staffeln,* one with He 70s, the other with He 45s.
AS/88	Naval reconnaissance *Staffel* with nine He 59 and one He 60 floatplanes.
B/88	Base-airfield operating company at the aircraft park.
F/88	Anti-aircraft detachment with four batteries of 88 mm guns and two batteries of 20 mm weapons.
J/88	Fighter *Gruppe* initially with three (occasionally four) *Staffeln* equipped with He 51s.
K/88	Bomber *Gruppe* initially with three (occasionally four) *Staffeln* equipped with Ju 52/3ms.
Laz/88	Field Hospital.
Ln/88	Signals battalion (with four companies).
MA/88	Ammunition depot.
P/88	Depot and aircraft supply *Abteilung.*
S/88	Operations staff.
San/88	Medical *Abteilung.*
VB/88	Experimental bomber *Staffel.*
VJ/88	Experimental fighter *Staffel.*
VS/88	Liaison staff to the Spanish and Italian forces.
W/88	Weather station.

The first of the new aircraft to arrive in Spain were twenty Ju 52/3ms for K/88 under *Major* Robert Fuchs, the machines flying from Greifswald by way of Rome and Melilla in Spanish Morocco to Sevilla. Henceforth four transport aircraft were dispatched to Spain from Germany each week and cargo boats were sent on average every five days. Included among the cargo of the latter were sixty He 51s for J/88 *(Jagdgruppe 88).* Commanded by *Major* Hubertus Merhardt von Bernegg, the unit comprised three *Staffeln*: 1.J/88 under *Hptm.* Werner Palm, 2.J/88 under *Oblt.* Otto Lehmann and 3.J/88 under *Oblt.* Jürgen Roth. After the *Gruppe* was assembled at Sevilla, the existing He 51 *Staffel* was redesignated 4.J/88.

Wolfram Freiherr von Richthofen seen here with the rank of General der Flieger and wearing the Ritterkreuz. When the Legion Condor went to Spain, von Richthofen was appointed Chief of Staff. Following several disagreements with the commander, Hugo Sperrle, he returned to Germany, only taking over command of the Legion Condor in December 1938.

The 4. *Staffel* shot down four enemy aircraft on 12 December and four days later 1.J/88 claimed its first victory. By now, however, the appearance of the new Russian fighters mentioned earlier ended a period of easy victories for the German pilots. Both the I-15 *"Chato"* and I-16 *"Rata"* fighters outclassed the He 51, and although Knüppel had scored eight victories, Eberhardt seven and Trautloft five by this time, relatively few successes were to be achieved during the first three months of 1937. At this time 3.J/88's pilots were quartered in a *Wohnzug* or housing train, a unique facility which comprised nine carriages with a steam locomotive at either end. Three carriages were used as sleeping quarters, two served as a mess hall, another as a kitchen, a seventh as a command centre and the remaining two as storage for spare parts. Aside from providing comfortable living quarters, the train had the useful advantage of being mobile.

RIGHT: A Heinkel He 70 reconnaissance aircraft of A/88 being escorted by two Italian Fiat C.R.32 fighters. The Fiat could hold its own with the early Russian aircraft that were sent to Spain and was far superior to the He 51.

BELOW: The first type of bomber used by the Legion Condor's bomber unit, Kampfgruppe *88*, was the Ju 52/3m. All such types carried the aircraft code "22".

BELOW AND RIGHT: Often known as a "Curtiss" by pilots of the Legion Condor, the Polikarpov I-15 "Chato" was one of the most successful biplane fighters, outclassing the He 51. Powered by a 700 hp M-25 radial engine, the I-15 possessed a maximum speed of 360 km/h (224 mph) and was highly manouvreable. It carried an armament of four 7.62 mm machine-guns.

Inferior in every aspect of performance to the Soviet fighters, the He 51 could also be easily outpaced by the fast new Tupolev SB-2 bomber. Another problem was that it possessed no radio, and its guns had to be manually cocked after each burst of fire. Fighter pilots, rather than protecting the bombers, were often forced to seek the shelter of their charges' guns. Distressed at their inability to fight on equal terms, *Major* Merhardt von Bernegg sought an interview with Sperrle at which he refused to send his pilots into the air against such overwhelming odds. He also warned that if he were directly ordered to do so he would demand to be relieved of his command and returned to Germany. The result of this unpleasant confrontation was that four prototype Bf 109s, the V3, V4, V5 and V6, plus the He 112 V3, were sent to VJ/88 in Spain early in December 1936. The Bf 109 V4 crashed, but Trautloft continued to test the other Messerschmitts and *Lt.* Günther Radusch the He 112.

Meanwhile the He 51s of J/88 were forced to operate as ground attack aircraft, a role in which they were to have some success. The unit also scored three aerial victories on 4 January 1937.

By early February 1937, 1.J/88 was at Escalona, 2.J/88 at Almorox, 3.J/88 at Villa del Prado and 4.J/88 at León. On 11 February, *Lt.* Rehanh was killed in an accident and next day, *Hptm.* Palm and *Lt.* Hepe were both shot down in flames, though they both managed to parachute to safety in friendly territory near Madrid.

ABOVE: At the end of the Spanish Civil War a number of victory parades were held in various Spanish cities. For one of these, held at Sanjurjo/Zaragoza, ten captured Republican I-16s were flown in to the city. Here, Oblt. Helmut-Felix Bolz of 3.J/88 (3 victories in Spain) stands in front of one of them.

RIGHT: With a maximum speed of 420 km/h (261 mph) at 5,000 m (16,500 ft) the Tupolev SB-2 Katiuska bomber was faster than Jagdgruppe 88's first fighter, the He 51. This aircraft was captured by the Nationalists and repainted in that air force's markings.

Messerschmitt Bf 109 V3

Flown by Oblt. Hannes Trautloft of VJ/88 from Sevilla/Tablada airfield, December 1936. This aircraft, W.Nr. 760, was one of four Bf 109 prototypes sent to Spain for testing under operational conditions, the others being the V4, V5 and V6. When flown by Trautloft, the V3 carried the "Green Heart" badge later used by JG 54 which he commanded from August 1940.

RIGHT: Hannes Trautloft (centre) standing in front of the Bf 109 V3 after delivery to Spain in December 1936. The aircraft had a large green heart painted below the cockpit.

BELOW: The poor performance of the He 51 in combat with the Republican I-15 and I-16 fighters led Germany to send prototypes of its newest fighters to Spain. The first Bf 109 prototype delivered was the V3 which arrived in December 1936. The code 6-1 was applied and the aircraft test flown by Oblt. Hannes Trautloft for the first time on 14 December from Sevilla-Tablada airfield. A total of four Bf 109 prototypes arrived in Spain, the V4 being destroyed in a take-off accident on 10 December 1936 with Uffz. Erwin Kley at the controls.

ABOVE: An close-up view of the two bladed wooden propeller as fitted to the Bf 109 B-1.

LEFT: The Bf 109 V4, D-IALY, was one of four prototypes of Messerschmitt's famous fighter to be sent to Spain. This aircraft was destroyed in a take-off accident on 10 December 1936, having been allocated the code 6-2 in Spain.

ABOVE: The He 112 V3 arrived in Spain in November 1936 where it was test flown by Oblt. Günther "Fips" Radusch. The prototype, which had been built without armament, had been fitted with an experimental engine-mounted 20 mm C/30 L cannon for tests. Shown here at Tablada airfield, the aircraft was given the code 5●1 and was later flown operationally against Republican armour by Uffz. Max Schulz of 1./J88 who destroyed three tanks.

RIGHT: A crowd of civilians watch as the engine of Lt. Ekkehard Hefter's He 51 fails just after take off from Vitoria during the transfer to Ávila on 28 September 1936. Shortly afterwards, the aircraft's left wing struck the tower of Vitoria town hall and Hefter crashed to his death. He was the first German pilot to be lost in the Spanish Civil War.

BELOW: The burning remains of Lt. Hefter's He 51 lie in front of Vitoria's Town Hall

One of my bitterest moments...

WOLF-HEINRICH *FREIHERR* VON HOUWALD

Wolf-Heinrich von Houwald was soon to discover that the He 51 was no match for the Russian fighters used by the Spanish Republican Air Force.

Wolf-Heinrich von Houwald entered the army on 1 April 1931, and transferred shortly afterwards to the *Deutsche Verkehrsfliegerschule* at Schleissheim where he learned to fly. Between 25 April and 3 June 1933 he was at Lipezk. He joined *Jagdgeschwader "Richthofen"* on 4 March 1935 and became one of the first six pilots to be sent to Spain. Von Houwald ended the Spanish Civil War with five victories. He later led II./JG 231 and then formed III./JG 52 and commanded this unit until he was shot down and killed on 24 July 1940.

"We arrived at Salamanca, the second stopping place on our way to Escalona, a small city near the Madrid Front. Salamanca was the first combat airfield I saw. We took a big chance in actually finding it because everything, including the aircraft, was very well camouflaged. We refuelled and took off for Escalona, an airfield that we heard was incredibly small and hard to find. It lay so close to the front that it was quite probable that we would engage the enemy. Nevertheless we found it after half an hour and landed. The airfield was so poor that we were worried whether our Spanish comrades would be able to fly our aircraft from there. Next day I had one of my most bitter moments. Full of enthusiasm and idealism, five Spaniards proudly climbed into our aircraft. They did not want foreigners to fight for them while they had to stay on the ground with nothing to do. But as they returned, my aircraft crashed on landing. Fortunately, the other Heinkels managed to land safely. From now on, without an aircraft, I had to stay on the ground while the others each shot down two or three enemy in short order. I had nothing better to do than to wait for new aircraft to come from *"Heimat"* (home). I kept thinking that they would arrive too late because the *Rojos* would be forced to surrender in front of Franco's massive offensive.

"On Friday 13 November 1936, we encountered the *Ratas* for the first time and a wild melee resulted. There were about 24 of them, only about nine of us. We shot down five of them, but what were these victories when compared with the loss of our *Staffelführer, Oblt.* Eberhardt and *Lt.* Henrici. Henrici had a brilliant career in front of him, having already shot down three enemy aircraft in one day. This only served to show that our good old He 51s were too slow compared with the new *Ratas* - they could play with us as they wanted. Furthermore the Soviet "Martin Bombers" which were arriving daily, were 50 km/h (30 mph) faster than us and the people were scared of them. Feverishly, we waited for the Bf 109s to arrive from Germany.

"Nevertheless, in spite of their technical advantage, the Soviet fighters had not attacked us with determination since 13 November. They respected us and the main target became our bombers which we had to escort. This also happened on the northern front when I was posted to 2.J/88 led by *Hptm.* Lehmann."

Taken from: *Das Buch der Spanien Flieger* (Editor: Hptm. Wulf Bley) v Hase & Köhler Verlag Leipzig, 1939

A line-up of the first He 51s to arrive in Spain pictured at Salamanca airfield. This photo was taken in early 1937 after the aircraft type code had been applied to "5".

A line up of a He 51s of J/88 probably photographed early in 1937.

The blackest day...

HERWIG KNÜPPEL

Knüppel gives the following account of the 13 November action: "The 13 November was the blackest day for the *Jagdstaffel Eberhardt.* We flew as escort for the bombers of *Oblt.* Rudolf von Moreau during the afternoon from Ávila to Madrid. After the second bombing run, we were attacked by 24 *Ratas* and *Curtisses* diving towards us from the east of Madrid at an altitude of between 1,200 and 1,500 m (4,000 and 5,000 ft). A major combat began. Eberhardt followed a biplane and shot it down but rammed his victim and they crashed locked together. So died our courageous *Staffelführer* who was much liked by all of his men as well as for his qualities as an officer. He had led our unit in an excellent manner and had shot down several enemy aircraft during his time in Spain.

There was another hard loss to bear when Oskar Henrici was hit in the spine. Despite his wounds, he shot down another biplane. He then landed behind our lines and was helped by Nationalist soldiers to climb from his aircraft. Nevertheless he died later. The rest of us fought hard and shot down several other aircraft. Among us, *Uffz.* Mratzek and Sawallisch were especially excellent. Also successful were *Lt.* von Gilsa (who was later killed in Spain), "Piefke" Strümpell and "Philipp" von Bothmer."

Modestly, Knüppel fails to mention that he shot down his seventh victim on this day.

Hptm. Herwig Knüppel (second from left) with Uffz. Erwin Sawallisch in front of the tail of a He 51 at Lacua (Vitoria) airfield, winter 1936. Knüppel was one of the first six German pilots to arrive in Spain in August. He took over command of 4.J/88 after Kraft Eberhardt was killed on 13 November 1936 and led the Staffel until 1 March 1937, gaining eight victories. Knüppel was killed on 19 May 1940 as Gruppenkommandeur of II./JG 26.

Taken from: *Das Buch der Spanien Flieger* (Editor: Hptm. Wulf Bley) v Hase & Köhler Verlag Leipzig, 1939

Detail of an early design of the Zylinderhut ("top hat") badge as shown on the He 51 below, coded 2●23.

BELOW: After the formation of Jagdgruppe *88*, the first German volunteer pilots in Spain were designated 4.J/88, and this was the first unit to adopt the "top hat" emblem.

ABOVE: A group of pilots preparing to go to Spain to serve with Jagdgruppe 88 including (from left): Lt. Wilhelm Ensslen (later with 9 victories who was awarded the Spanienkreuz in Gold mit Brillanten, later killed during the Second World War), Hptm. Jürgen Roth, Lt. Karl Ebbighausen (3 victories) and Lt. Günther Scholz (1 victory).

ABOVE: The "Zylinderhut" (top hat) insignia was first carried by the He 51s of 4.J/88 before being passed to the Bf 109s of 2.J/88 when the former Staffel was disbanded. It commemorated the antics of a Luftwaffe officer, who had just left the army, and was spotted wearing a top hat instead of his service cap. This became a standing joke within the Luftwaffe. Here the badge appears on a board indicating 2.J/88's accomodation area. Note the alternative presentation of the unit designation.

LEFT: Two He 51s with Oblt. Dietrich "Philipp" von Bothmer standing in the foreground. Von Bothmer had two victories in Spain: a Curtiss on 13 November 1936 (the Legion Condor's 29th kill) and a Rata on 8 December 1936 (the 32nd kill).

Heinkel He 51 B-1 of 4.J/88
Based at Ávila, November 1936. With the arrival of the Legion Condor in Spain, the first German fighter unit was redesignated 4.J/88, but the finish and markings of its He 51s changed little. This aircraft has the "top hat" badge painted on the fuselage sides, the marking later being passed to 2.J/88 after the 4. Staffel was disbanded in March 1937.

Detail of the "top hat" badge as shown on the He 51 above. Note the minor differences to those shown opposite.

ABOVE AND LEFT: Before and after! Two photographs of a He 51 B-1 of 4.J/88 before and after the top hat emblem was applied to the fuselage sides. There were several variations of this emblem, examples of which were used on Luftwaffe fighters during the Second World War.

LEFT: A group of NCO pilots from 3./J88 shows (from left to right): Uffz. Peter Keller, Uffz. Josef Bauer (3 victories), Uffz. Boer (1 victory), Uffz. Kienig (1 victory), Uffz. Waldemar Gestermann and Uffz. Franz Jaenisch (1 victory).

ABOVE: Heinrich Ehrler in civilian clothes with the Spanish flag in the background. Ehrler served in Spain as an Unteroffizier in Flak/88, the Legion Condor's anti-aircraft unit. He was killed in action before the end of the Second World War as a fighter pilot with the rank of Major having accumulated 208 victories. As Kommodore of JG 5, he was held in disgrace, having been responsible for the sinking of the battleship Tirpitz and was transferred to JG 7 flying the Me 262.

ABOVE: This He 51 does not appear to carry any national markings beneath the wings. An unusual feature sometimes used was the painting of large white diagonal crosses beneath the wings whereas the usual practice was for this to be painted on the black circle national insignia.

RIGHT: The first Staffelkapitän of 1.J/88, Oblt. Werner Palm standing beside a Mercedes truck with a He 51 in the background. It is interesting to note that even at this time the Heinkel has camouflage applied, and also that the Nationalist insignia has been painted on the mudguard of the truck.

Der Reichsminister der Luftfahrt und
Oberbefehlshaber der Luftwaffe

Der am 13. November 1936 in Gegend Mosteles erfolgte
Abschuß eines Flugzeuges, Typ Doppeldecker wird dem

Leutnant
Dietrich v. Bothmer

als 1. Luftsieg

bestätigt.

Berlin, den 21. April 1938.

Generalfeldmarschall

Der Reichsminister der Luftfahrt und
Oberbefehlshaber der Luftwaffe

Der am 8. Dezember 1936 in Gegend Vitoria
erfolgte Abschuß eines Flugzeuges, Typ Curtiß, wird dem

Leutnant
Dietrich v. Bothmer

als 2. Luftsieg

bestätigt.

Berlin, den 6. Juni 1939.

Generalfeldmarschall

Just after this photo was taken at Ávila on 13 November 1936, Oblt. Kraft Eberhardt (centre) was killed when his He 51 collided with a Republican fighter. His place as Kapitän of 4.J/88 was taken by Herwig Knüppel. To the left of this photo is Lt. Dietrich von Bothmer with Lt. Hennig Strümpell to the right.

RIGHT: Wolfram von Richthofen (standing in the group nearest the camera, holding binoculars) watching an operation by the Legion Condor with a number of German and Spanish officers.

BELOW: The ruins of the Basque town of Guernica hit by bombs dropped by aircraft from the German bomber unit, Kampfgruppe 88 on 26 April 1937. The intended target for the attack was a railway station and bridge outside the town, but because of poor visibility the town itself was hit, resulting in the death of over 300 civilians. Guernica was to become synonymous with the indiscrimate bombing of innocent civilians and became the subject of one of Pablo Picasso's most famous paintings.

MARCH TO OCTOBER 1937

The Messerschmitt Bf 109 arrives

On 14 March 1937, the first three Bf 109 B-1s were delivered to 2.J/88. Although possessing a much improved performance over the He 51, the early Messerschmitts suffered continuous problems with their Jumo 210 engines. In addition they still had fixed pitch wooden propellers and the manually cocked machine-guns. The He 51s released from 2.J/88 were transferred to Spanish units, but 1. and 3.J/88 continued to operate the type for some time. 4.J/88 was disbanded during the middle of the month, its now famous top hat insignia being transferred to 2.J/88.

The lack of success around Madrid led Franco to switch direction and attempt to take the strip of Basque territory along the northern coast between Gijon and Bilbao. For this operation, J/88 was transferred to Vitoria and, simultaneously, aircraft were shipped to Vigo instead of Cadiz. The offensive began on 31 March, the main thrust being directed towards the Ochandiano-Bilbao area. The He 51s of 1. and 3.J/88 flew continuous sorties in support of the ground forces, the Spaniards nicknaming them *Cadenas* (Chains) from the way aircraft returned again and again to the same target. At this time 3.J/88 was led by *Oblt.* Douglas Pitcairn, a direct descendant of a family from Perthshire in Scotland.

Having re-equipped with the Messerschmitt Bf 109, 2.J/88 flew against the Republican fighters with confidence, its first victory with the new type occurring on 6 April when *Oblt.* Günther Lützow shot down a "Curtiss". The Bf 109, especially the B-2 model with its Hamilton variable pitch metal propeller, was to prove superior to most Republican fighters and at least equal to the I-16.

Later in the offensive, on 26 April, the Legion Condor attempted to bomb a bridge at Guernica, but succeeded only in hitting the town and killing over 300 people. On 27 April Marquina fell, followed by Guernica two days later. On 1 May, Bilbao was encircled, the "Iron Ring" around the city being reached six days later. The He 51s flew a large number of sorties during the battle for the heights near Amorebieta and the hill of Bizcargui which dominated the surrounding area. During the actions against ground troops, the He 112 V3 with its 20 mm engine-mounted cannon, often operated against Republican tanks. It was usually piloted by *Uffz.* Max Schulz of 1.J/88 and acquired the descriptive nickname *"Dosenöffner"* (Can Opener). Finally, on 19 June, Bilbao was taken.

While the battle for the north raged, the Republicans launched an offensive at Brunete, 24 km (15 miles) west of Madrid on 6 July 1937. Their aim was to break through the Nationalist lines at their weakest point. Returning to their old airfield at Salamanca-Matacán, 2.J/88 made an immediate impact on the Republican air forces who, up to that time, were not aware of the arrival of the Bf 109 in Spain. Often operating in temperatures of around 50 °C (120 °F), several massive air battles took place, sometimes involving as many as 200 aircraft. Gradually the Nationalists forced the attackers back to their starting point, the Republicans losing 20,000 of their best troops in the process. In the air, 104 Communist aircraft were lost against 23 on the Nationalist side.

The first Bf 109 B-1 sent to Spain was 6-3, seen here wearing the "top hat" emblem of 2.J/88. This photograph was taken at Herrera de Pisuerga airfield when the Staffel recuperated following months of heavy combat operations. The aircraft in the background, coded 30-3, is a RWD-13 "Polaca" single-engined liaison aircraft.

Adolf Galland (smoking his familiar cigar) arrived in Spain on 8 May 1937 but did not begin operational flying until 24 July. He officially led 3.J/88 between 27 July 1937 and 24 May 1938 when Werner Mölders took over. Galland and Mölders became friends but also opponents in the victory-race during the Battle of Britain. Their tally was not to be compared in Spain due to Galland's Staffel being equipped with the old He 51 flying ground attack sorties. Just after Mölders arrived, 3.J/88 was re-equipped with the Bf 109 which enabled him to claim no fewer than 14 victories. Galland is seen here in his command-train with the Staffel's Mickey Mouse insignia. This train followed the crews as they changed airfields. As an experienced ground attack pilot, Galland led 4.(S)/LG 2 during the campaign against Poland. Note that although Mölders was the top scoring German pilot with 14 kills, his Spanish counterpart, Joaquin Garcia Morato, had 40!

In April 1937, Oblt. Douglas Pitcairn (left) and Oblt. Harro Harder arrived in Spain to take over command of 3. and 1.J/88 respectively. Both units were still equipped with the He 51, the first Bf 109s having been just delivered to the 2.Staffel. Pitcairn survived the Second World War although he was injured on 5 August 1940 during the Battle of Britain. Harder undertook a second tour of duty in Spain, testing the He 112 V9 with 2. Staffel but was killed on 12 August 1940 in the "Battle of Britain".

One of the most successful days for 2.J/88 came on 12 July when it shot down six aircraft. Next day, three more I-16s were destroyed and the *Staffel* claimed another five Republican aircraft up to the end of the month. One of these, on 16 July, was the fifth victory scored by *Lt.* Pingel, an I-16 over Aranjuez. The successes were not without cost, *Oblt.* Lützow reporting on 21 July that he only had three serviceable Messerschmitts left.

Meanwhile 1. and 3.J/88 with the He 51 flew continuous ground support operations around Brunete. On 24 July, for example, the *1. Staffel* flew three sorties, each aircraft carrying six 10 kg (22 lb) bombs, but lost *Lt.* Reuter shot down by *Flak*. These pioneering ground support operations were largely evolved by *Oberst* von Richthofen who often positioned himself on a hill overlooking the battle area and informed the He 51s of suitable targets by telephone - the aircraft having no radio equipment. Just prior to this, on 19 July, the He 112 V3 was finally written off when it crashed following engine trouble. The aircraft had destroyed three tanks.

In August, the Legion Condor returned to the northern front, the three *Staffeln* of J/88 moving to Alar del Reyand Callahorra. At this time, 1. and 3.J/88 possessed eighteen He 51s and nine Bf 109s. Operating in the Santander area, the He 51s again flew continuous attacks on road and rail targets and against Republican troops, moving to the forward airfield at Orzales on 18 August. Meanwhile, 2.J/88 increased its reputation as a squadron of *experten* when, on 17 August, three more enemy aircraft were destroyed, two by *Fw.* Peter Boddem. Another three were shot down on the 18th, one (an I-15 over Santander) giving *Fw.* Boddem his eighth victory, all scored in just over a month.

On 25 August Santander fell, around 50,000 Republican prisoners and a large amount of war material passing into Nationalist hands. By this time, 1.J/88 had begun converting to the Bf 109 B, *Oblt.* Harro Harder claiming the *Staffel's* first victory with the type on 27 August, a Tupolev SB-2. While Nationalist troops concentrated on mopping up operations, the Republicans gathered 80,000 men at Belchite south of Zaragoza for an assault on the city. By 26 August, Zaragoza was seriously threatened and the He 51s of 3.J/88, now under *Oblt.* Adolf Galland, were rushed to the area and heavily committed. Some of the unit's Heinkels had the popular Mickey Mouse cartoon character painted on their sides but this had been introduced by Pitcairn's mechanics, not Galland as widely thought. Apart from conventional bombs, 3.J/88 also operated with two fragmentation bombs tied to their 170 litre fuselage drop tanks. It was found that when this was dropped, it exploded on impact, showering enemy troops with burning fuel, a forerunner, perhaps, of the infamous Napalm.

By 9 September, the Republican offensive against Zaragoza had petered out. Previously, on 1 September, Franco had launched a drive into Asturia with the aim of taking its capital city Gijon and overrunning the one remaining enemy enclave in the north. *Oblt.* Harder was particularly successful during this period, claiming his third victory on 7 September, two more on the 9th and a sixth on the 15th. On 27 September, three more *Ratas* were shot down, two by Harder, with a further one to follow next day. By 13 October, he claimed his tenth victim, bringing him level with Boddem. Meanwhile, 3.J/88 continued its ground attack operations, and during one notable operation, set a huge fuel dump at Gijon on fire. On 21 September, the unit moved to the coastal city of Llanes which had only recently been captured, harrying the Republican troops as they retreated west. On 21 October, Nationalist forces entered Gijon and the Republican northern front effectively collapsed, 150,000 prisoners falling into Franco's hands.

By the summer of 1937, many Legion Condor aircraft had begun to adopt camouflaged uppersurfaces, various combinations of brown and green being used. Also by this time, the He 51s had been relegated to the ground attack role. The aircraft at the back is a He 45 which was sometimes also used to drop bombs on ground troops. The He 51 third from the right is coded 2●62 and carries a derivative of the "Marabu" badge on the starboard side of the fuselage.

March to October 1937

LEFT: After proving inadequate as a fighter, the He 51 was switched to the ground support role in Spain where it was used to develop "ground attack" tactics which were later adopted by the Luftwaffe during the Second World War. This aircraft coded 2●62 caries a stylized "Marabu" badge on the starboard side of the fuselage, which was probably also repeated on the port side.

RIGHT: On 19 July 1937, the He 112 V3, piloted by Uffz. Schulz or "Dosen Max" as he was nicknamed, suffered an engine failure just short of the airfield at Escalona. Although he managed to belly land the aircraft, it broke its back on impact and was written off. Schulz himself escaped with injuries to his tongue which he almost bit through.

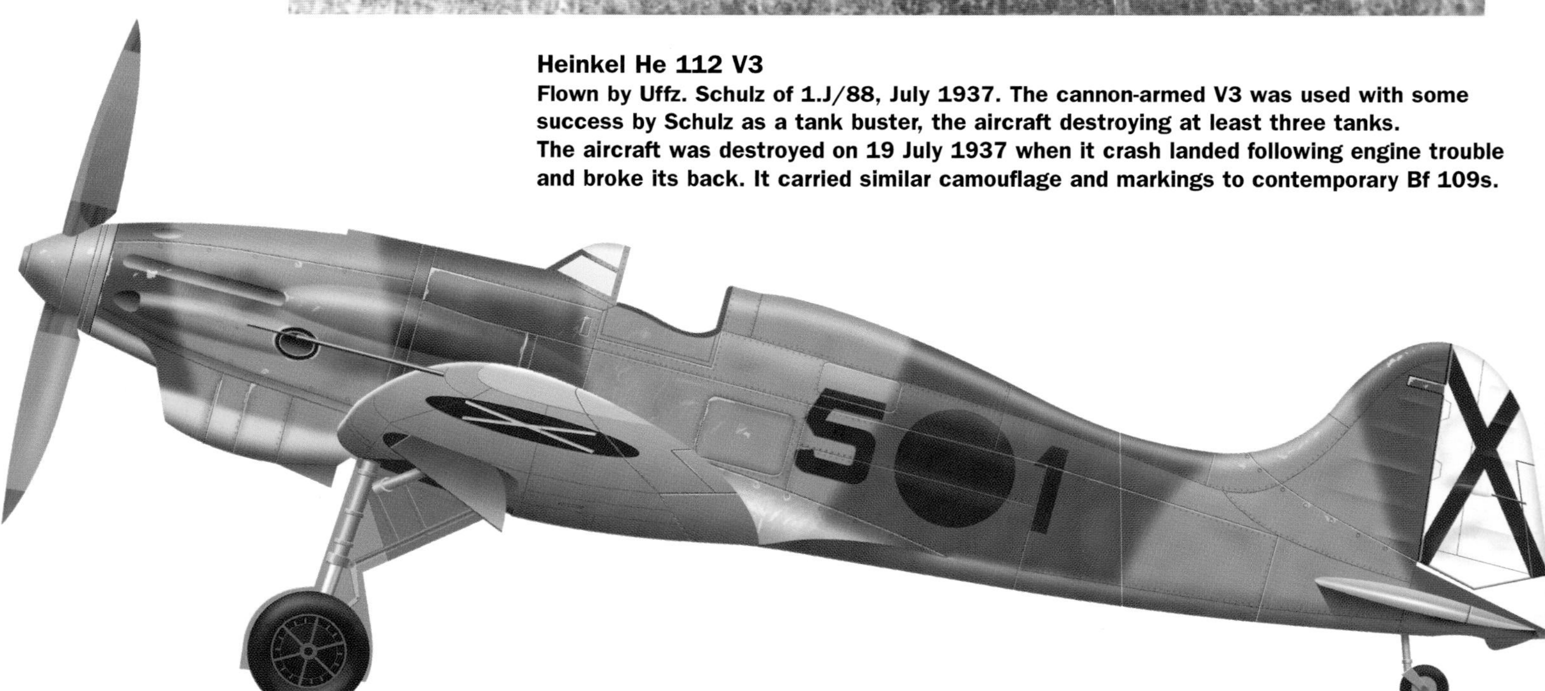

Heinkel He 112 V3

Flown by Uffz. Schulz of 1.J/88, July 1937. The cannon-armed V3 was used with some success by Schulz as a tank buster, the aircraft destroying at least three tanks. The aircraft was destroyed on 19 July 1937 when it crash landed following engine trouble and broke its back. It carried similar camouflage and markings to contemporary Bf 109s.

Heinkel He 51 B-1

Flown by Oblt. Harro Harder, Staffelkapitän of 1.J/88, summer 1937. Because it was increasingly used for ground attack, it was found necessary to improve the aircraft's camouflage with the addition of dark green patches. The aircraft carries the "Marabu" (Marabou) badge of 1.J/88 reminiscent of the popular German cartoon character "Hans Huckebein". Harder's use of the Hakenkreuz (swastika) emblem was officially frowned upon, and some of his later aircraft carried a simple diagonal cross in the same position.

"Marabu" (Marabou) badge

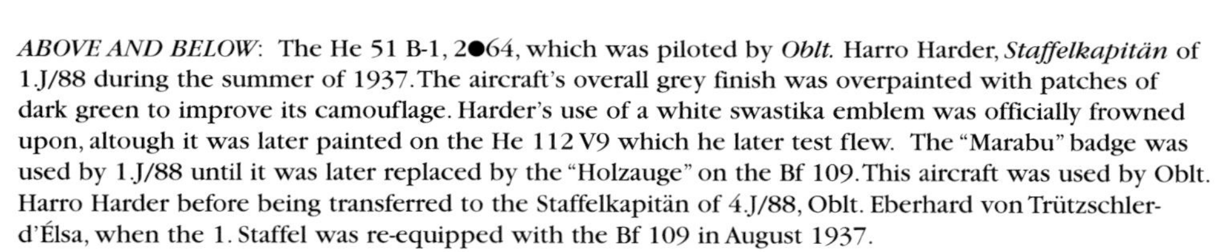

ABOVE AND BELOW: The He 51 B-1, 2●64, which was piloted by *Oblt.* Harro Harder, *Staffelkapitän* of 1.J/88 during the summer of 1937.The aircraft's overall grey finish was overpainted with patches of dark green to improve its camouflage. Harder's use of a white swastika emblem was officially frowned upon, altough it was later painted on the He 112 V9 which he later test flew. The "Marabu" badge was used by 1.J/88 until it was later replaced by the "Holzauge" on the Bf 109.This aircraft was used by Oblt. Harro Harder before being transferred to the Staffelkapitän of 4.J/88, Oblt. Eberhard von Trützschler-d'Élsa, when the 1. Staffel was re-equipped with the Bf 109 in August 1937.

ABOVE: Armed Spanish Civil Guards patrol in front of a He 51 biplane fighter.

March to October 1937

ABOVE: Probably taken during the heavy fighting that took place at the battle of Brunete, this photo shows several He 51s which flew continuous ground attack sorties. In the foreground can be seen 2●62.

BELOW: Adolf Galland's first aircraft in Spain after taking over command of 3.J/88 in July 1937 was 2●10. The aircraft is shown here after a landing mishap when it flipped over on to its back. He later flew 2●78 which is illustrated on page 143.

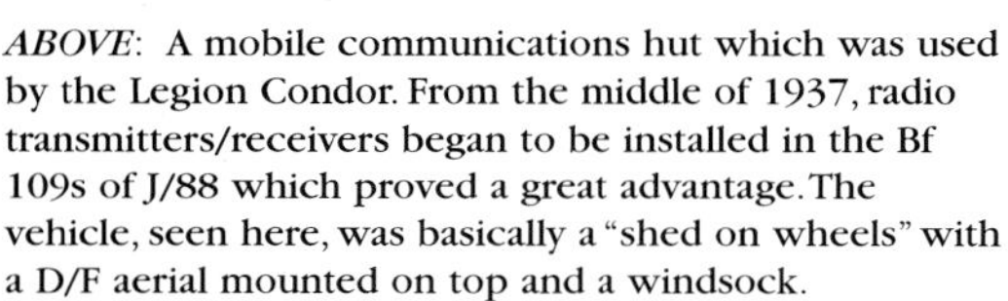

ABOVE: A mobile communications hut which was used by the Legion Condor. From the middle of 1937, radio transmitters/receivers began to be installed in the Bf 109s of J/88 which proved a great advantage. The vehicle, seen here, was basically a "shed on wheels" with a D/F aerial mounted on top and a windsock.

RIGHT: A group of pilots photographed at Santander during the summer of 1937. Many of the pilots shown here went on to achieve fame during the Second World War. From left to right are: Gotthard Handrick (commander of J/88), Peter Boddem (10 victories in Spain), Günther Lützow (Kapitän of 2.J/88), Joachim Schlichting (partially hidden and next leader of 2.J/88), Walter Ehle, Harro Harder (Kapitän of 1.J/88), Erich Woitke and Rolf Pingel.

RIGHT: A total of twenty-seven Bf 109 B-2s were delivered to the Legion Condor in Spain, coded 6●19 to 6●45. Only five C-1s (numbered 6●46 to 6●50) were sent to Spain, the type differing in being powered by a Jumo 210 Ga engine with direct fuel injection. This gave it a slightly improved performance over the B-series.

LEFT AND BELOW: One of the first Bf 109s being unloaded in Spain at Tablada in 1936 after delivery from Germany. All fighters were sent to Spain by ship as the fighter aircraft lacked the range to be flown in from Italy like many of the Legion Condor's bombers.

LEFT: Later versions of the Bf 109 B were fitted with a two blade variable pitch metal propeller of American design. The original variants with wooden propellers were retrospectively modified. This photo shows maintenance work being carried out on the aircraft's Jumo 210 engine.

LEFT: This Fieseler Fi 156 A Storch made an emergency landing on one of J/88's airfields. The type was allocated the aircraft type code "46" in Spain.

RIGHT: The first production Bf 109 B-1 sent to Spain being overhauled. As far as is known, although four Bf 109 prototypes were tested by Versuchsverband J/88 of the Legion Condor, only the first two (the V3 and V4) were given aircraft code numbers (respectively 6-1 and 6-2)

LEFT: The same Bf 109 B-1 as shown above, later on in the war after it had been converted to a B-2 variant, with a two bladed variable pitch metal propeller. At this time the aircraft had also been re-painted in medium green (62) and the code 6●3 re-applied in the new fatter style numbers.

RIGHT: An early Bf 109 carrying the "top hat" insignia of 2.J/88 taxies towards the runway. This aircraft, coded 6-4, was possibly the V6 which was tested in Spain. It was painted overall pale grey with black and white national insignia.

LEFT: Fw. Herbert Ihlefeld seen in the cockpit of his Bf 109 B-1 coded 6●6 following his sixth victory on 25 June 1938. Ihlefeld, who was later promoted to Leutnant in Spain, was to become one of the Jagdwaffe's leading personalities, claiming 101 victories and ending the war as Kommodore of JG 1.

Detail of "top hat" badge on Ihlefeld's Bf 109.

Messerschmitt Bf 109 B-1

This aircraft was flown by Fw. Herbert Ihlefeld of 2./J.88, June 1938. It was one of the first Bf 109 B-1s to arrive in Spain and had its wooden propeller replaced by a Hamilton metal unit. At the same time the code "6-6" (separated by a hyphen) was modified to the later style with the numbers positioned either side of the black circle national insignia.

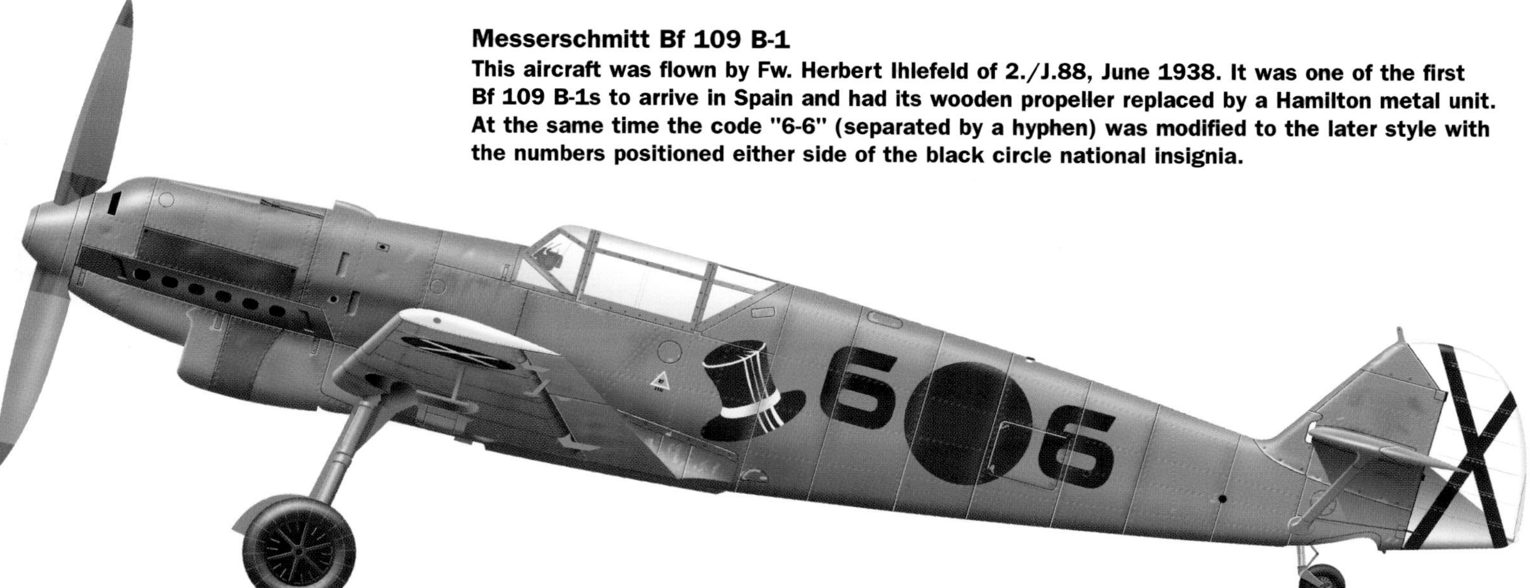

ABOVE: Photographed at Escratón airfield during the Aragón offensive, this group of Bf 109 B-1s carry the later style of marking system, with the aircraft type number forward of the black national insignia circle and the individual number aft. Previously Bf 109s had both numbers painted behind the circle, with a hyphen between. 6●6 in the foreground was flown by Fw. Herbert Ihlefeld before being written off by Uffz. Franz Jaenisch in July 1938. It has had the wooden propeller replaced by a Hamilton metal unit.

March to October 1937

RIGHT: A Bf 109 B-1 in flight over Spanish mountains.

RIGHT: An early production Bf 109 B-1 (which had a wooden propeller) probably photographed at Escatrón airfield during the Aragón offensive. The last B-1 to be sent to Spain was 6●18, later aircraft being of the B-2 sub-type with the Hamilton metal variable pitch propeller.

BELOW: This early Bf 109 B-1, piloted by Fw. Norbert Fliegel, crashed on takeoff from Santander-West airfield. Santander was positioned on a gentle slope which often caused problems on take-off and landing.

ABOVE: Two Bf 109 B-1s with the "Zylinder Hut" (top hat) emblem painted on the sides of their fuselages. The emblem was introduced very early on in the Spanish campaign by 4.J/88 and later passed to the 2. Staffel after the former was disbanded in March 1937.

LEFT: Many of the Bf 109 B-1s had their original two bladed fixed wooden propellers replaced by a two bladed variable pitch Hamilton Metal unit, of US design, which gave a marked improvement to the performance of the aircraft.

BELOW: Following the successful testing of the Bf 109 prototypes, a batch of B-1 production aircraft were delivered to 2.J/88 at Almorox. Despite possessing a much improved performance over the He 51, the B-1 model had a fixed-pitch wooden propeller and carried an armament of only two manually cocked machine-guns.

ABOVE: The Bf 109 B-1 flown by Oblt. Günther Lützow, Staffelkapitän of 2.J/88, the first unit to be equipped with the aircraft in Spain. When they arrived, in March 1937, the aircraft proved at least equal to the best Republican fighters, but suffered continuous problems with their Jumo 210 engines.

RIGHT: Making an interesting comparison with the photo above, this picture shows Günther Lützow's Bf 109 B after being fitted with a metal variable pitch propeller. Note that the marking style has been changed and the top hat badge added.

BELOW: Uffz. Hermann Stange's aircraft, coded 6-12, after suffering a crash landing at Santander-West airfield. Stange was to shoot down three Republican aircraft in Spain, but probably received a dressing down for the mishap shown here!

RIGHT: When the Bf 109 B-1 entered service in Spain still with its Schwarz fixed-pitch wooden propeller, it was seriously under-gunned. It carried an armament of only two 7.9 mm MG 17 machine-guns above the engine cowling and these had to be manually cocked after each burst.

ABOVE AND RIGHT: This Bf 109 B-1, coded 6-15, was piloted by Uffz. Otto Polenz of 1.J/88 who was captured on 4 December 1937 on the Aragon front at Corta Azaila-Escatron. The aircraft was later evaluated by a French commission before being shipped to the USSR.

March to October 1937

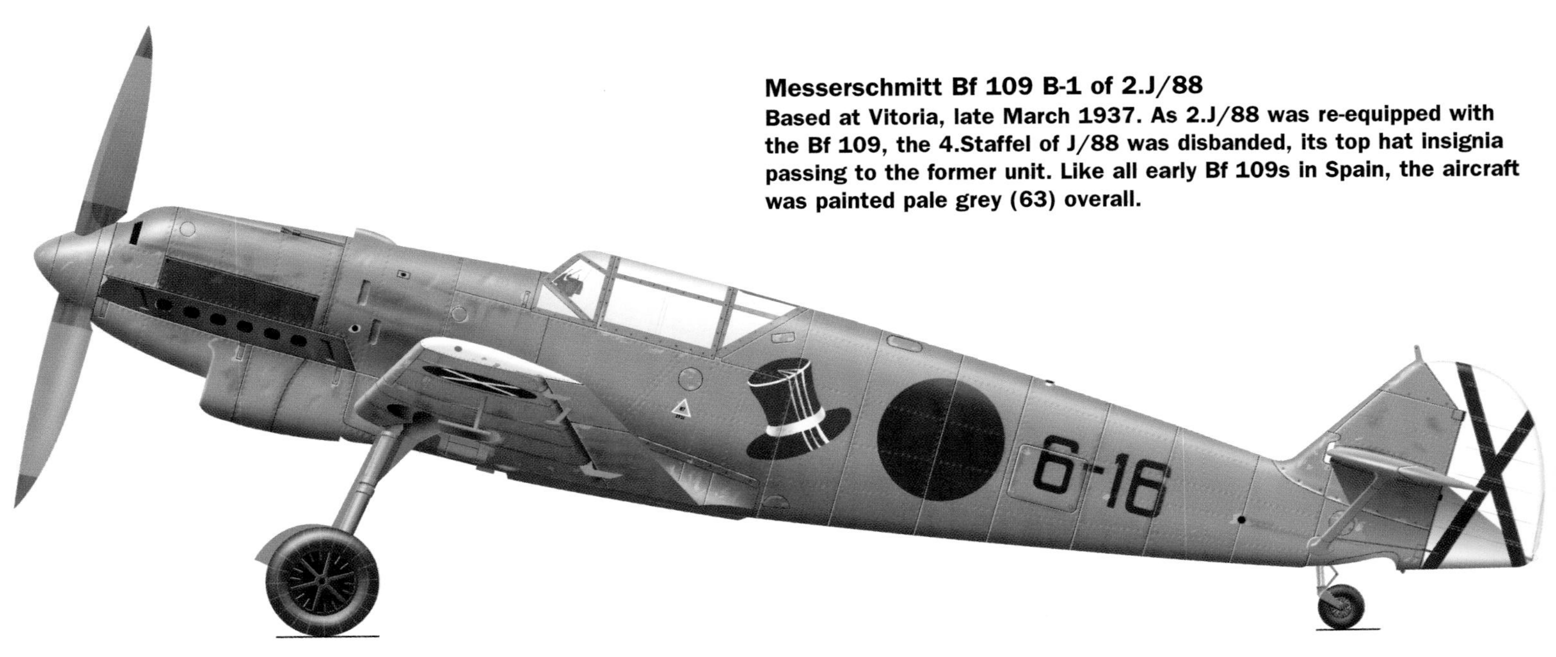

Messerschmitt Bf 109 B-1 of 2.J/88

Based at Vitoria, late March 1937. As 2.J/88 was re-equipped with the Bf 109, the 4.Staffel of J/88 was disbanded, its top hat insignia passing to the former unit. Like all early Bf 109s in Spain, the aircraft was painted pale grey (63) overall.

RIGHT: Illustrated above in colour, this Bf 109 B-1 shows the typical smoke blackening from the Jumo 210 engine which often extended from the exhaust along the fuselage sides as far as the wing trailing edge. The top hat emblem was later also adopted by several Luftwaffe Staffeln during World War Two.

BELOW: A variety of aircraft photographed in León airfield in Spain. Nearest the camera is a Bf 109 B-1 coded 6●16 with a Ju 86, a captured Vultee V-1A transport and a Do 17 behind. Codes 6-1 to 6-2 were allocated to the Bf 109 V3 and V4 prototypes, 6-3 to 6-18 to Bf 109 B-1 production aircraft, codes 6-19 to 6-45 to Bf 109 B-2s, codes 6-46 to 6-50 to Bf 109 C-1s, 6-51 to 6-86 to Bf 109 D-1s and 6-87 to 6-131 to Bf 109 E-1 and E-3s.

Uffz. Wilhelm Staege begins his take-off run in his Bf 109 B-2 at Alar d'el Rey during the summer of 1937.

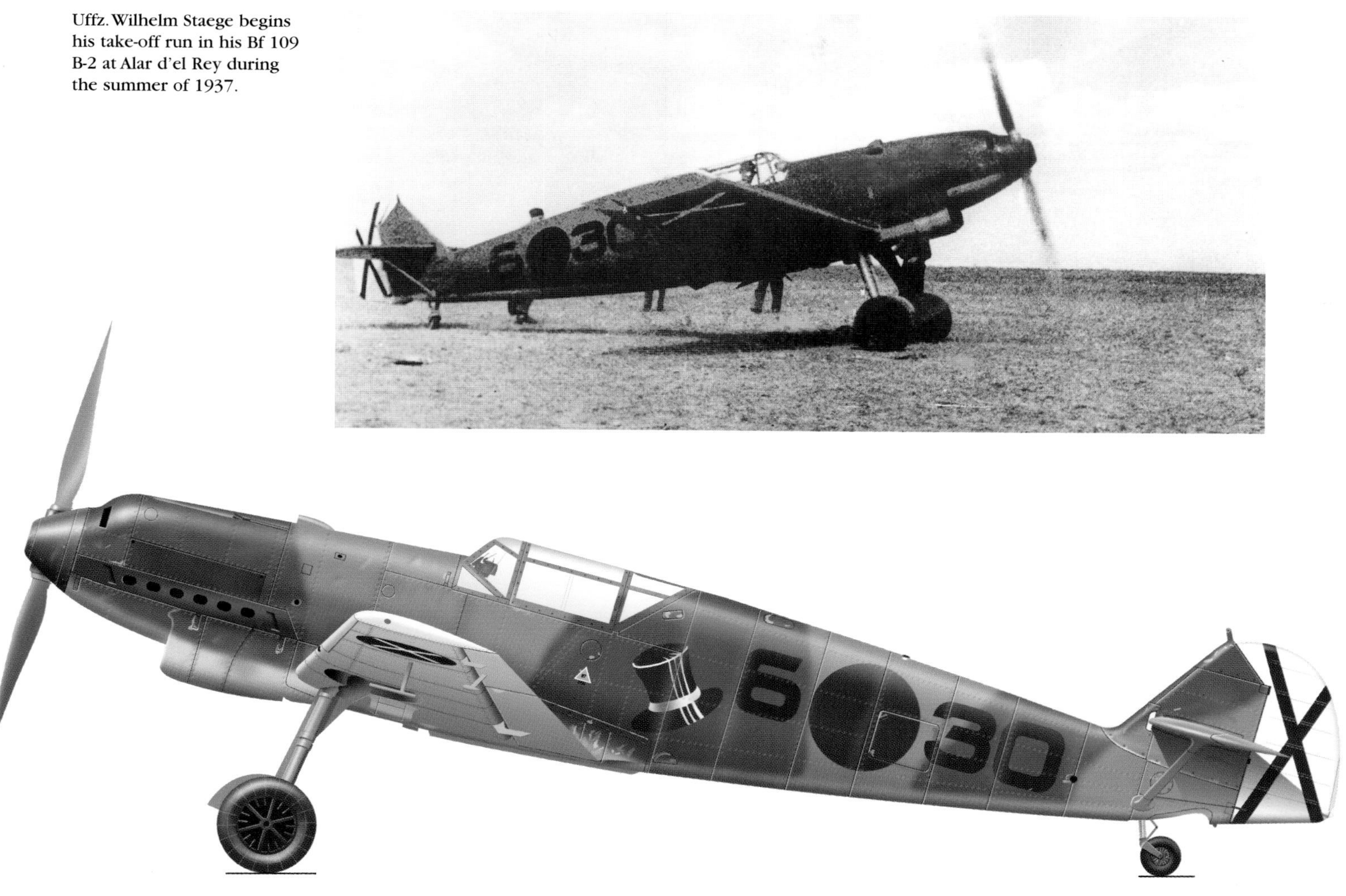

Messerschmitt Bf 109 B-2

Flown by Uffz. Wilhelm Staege of 2.J/88, Alar d'el Rey, July 1937. This aircraft cartwheeled on landing and ended up on its back, but Staege was pulled from the wreckage with only minor injuries. By this time, Bf 109s in Spain had adopted a camouflage pattern of pale grey (RLM colour 63) and medium green (62) uppersurfaces with pale blue (65) beneath.

This Bf 109 B-2, coded 6●30, crashed on landing and flipped over on to its back at Alar d' el Rey airfield in July 1937. The aircraft was piloted by Uffz. Wilhelm Staege of 2.J/88 who was pulled from the wreckage with minor injuries. Staege claimed three victories in Spain.

ABOVE: Three German pilots greet each other in Spain. From left to right: Lt. Lommel, unknown, Oblt. Hans Schmoller-Haldy, Lt. Josef Fözö. "Joschko" Fözö, with 3.J/88, scored three victories in Spain. He was later to command II./JG 51 and was awarded the Ritterkreuz on 2 July 1941.

ABOVE: In July 1937 Lt. Peter Boddem of the 2.Staffel of J/88 shot down two I-16s and later reached a total of 10 aircraft, putting him fourth in the list of German aces in Spain. He was awarded the Spanienkreuz in Gold mit Brillanten (Spanish Cross in Gold with Diamonds), but was killed as a passenger in a Ju 52 crash on his way back from Spain after his second "tour" of operations. At the time of his death he was in fact listed as one of the first losses of JG 26, as he had been posted to this Geschwader. This aircraft carried the top hat badge below the rear part of the cockpit.

RIGHT: A Bf 109 B-2 coded 6●32, of J/88 undergoing machine-gun calibration tests.

LEFT: Loaded with bombs or equipped with heavy machine-guns, the He 59 "Zapatones" flew aggressive patrols or attacks against enemy harbours. The first five He 59s arrived at the end of 1936 and were delivered to AS/88. Around twenty of the type were used in Spain, its main success being the sinking of the battleship Jamie I in Almeria harbour on the night of 24/25 May 1937. Seven or so He 59s were lost in the fighting in Spain and about five survived to serve with the Spanish Navy into the later 1940s.

RIGHT: Four Ju 87 As were sent to Spain to evaluate the new dive bomber. The unit which operated them was known as the "Jolanthe Kette" after a cartoon pig character, this temporarily operating under J/88 as its 5.Staffel.

BELOW: The "Jolanthe" emblem, a pink sow on a white oval, was painted on the outside of the undercarriage spats of the four Ju 87s that were delivered to Spain. For a short time the unit that operated the aircraft was known as 5.J/88 before being attached to the Legion Condor's bomber Gruppe, K/88.

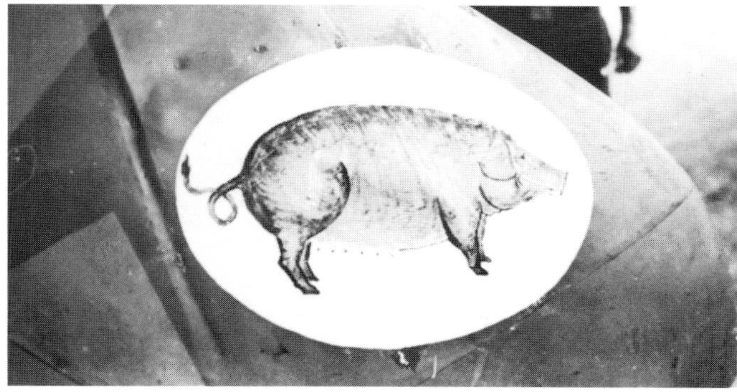

I knew I would not be able to reach my lines...

FRITZ LOSIGKEIT

"On 22 February 1938, while serving with 2./JG 132 *"Richthofen"*, I was transferred to Bernburg airfield, northwest of Leipzig where the unit's pilots underwent advanced combat training. This was, in essence, the operational training and readiness element of the *Geschwader*. I had not been there very long before I was contacted by a senior officer who wanted to know if I would agree to go to Spain and fight with the Legion Condor. My long service career and the fact that I was not married, made me a perfect candidate. I was, of course, very excited at the prospect of going to Spain and volunteered. My spirits were very high because my *Staffelkapitän* had been to Spain for about a year and returned to us with many exciting stories.Apart from the opportunity of gaining valuable front-line experience, there was also a political motivation; we all thought that the Communists would seize control of Spain and we wanted to keep the Spanish free.

"I arrived at Zaragoza on 25 March 1938, where I was attached to 3.J/88, a *Staffel* equipped with the He 51 and specialising in ground attack operations. When I arrived in Spain, the unit's *Staffelkapitän*, Adolf Galland, was about to return to Germany. He left *Oblt.* Lehrmann in command, who was assisted by *Oblt.* Werner Mölders.

"Some of J./88's pilots had already claimed many victories, especially those in the *1. and 2. Staffeln*; Harder had 11 "kills", Boddem, 10, Seiler, 9 and Balthasar, 6 and so on. Our *3. Staffel* was still equipped with the old He 51 which could only operate on a defensive basis in combat against the famous *"Rata"*. We were thus assigned ground attack duties against enemy positions in the Lerida area. However, since my arrival, I had noted how Mölders worked hard to try to exchange our He 51s for the Bf 109 which was already in use by the other *Staffeln*.

"Most of our missions could not be considered dangerous, since there was no anti-aircraft defence and the enemy infantry had very little chance of hitting us with small arms fire. Nevertheless, on 31 May 1938, I took off in the afternoon for my second mission of the day, a mission which would prove to be my last in Spain. *Oblt.* Lehrmann led the *Staffel* with *Oblt.* Mölders leading my *Schwarm*. We were briefed to attack an artillery position close to the front. After about 15 minutes, I saw a dusty cloud in the area of our target and as I approached, I could see that it was a truck. Because, it was so near the front and close to enemy lines, I assumed it was carrying munitions. The truck was moving fast and I very soon realised that he was actually making for the cover of the enemy defences. My first attack was unsuccessful and I decided to approach the truck at the lowest possible altitude. Then I neared it, a 2 cm four-barreled *Flak* gun opened fire. I was taken completely by surprise and my aircraft was hit at an altitude of 100 metres (300 feet).

"Fortunately, I was not wounded but my aircraft was so badly damaged that I knew I would not be able to reach my lines. I quickly decided to bail out. Seconds after opening the parachute, I hit the ground. In the meantime, my comrades, having seen me shot down, opened fire in order to discourage the enemy from attempting to pick me up. In fact, having released my parachute, they could see exactly where I was and that I was still alive.

"I was captured almost immediately. The eight months that followed my capture were the worst in my entire military career. I was often beaten up by the jailers, who viewed me not as a soldier but as a rebel. One morning I was summoned twice to be confronted with a firing squad.

"Then I was sent to a prison in Valencia where I was given my first drink in ten days. I was continually questioned and, after several weeks, I was flown to Barcelona. I then followed in the footsteps of my retreating captors (members of the Communist Spanish air arm) to Catalonia and finally to the Pyrenees. At the end of the year, my captors decided to cross the Pyrenees and seek refuge in France. It was not, of course, an easy matter to cross these mountains during the winter after having been weakened by such long and harsh captivity, but to almost feel freedom - to see it beyond the mountains - gave me a new energy. Another danger arose from the fact that the Pyrenees were constantly being patrolled for deserters. Several times, I was close to being captured again, but I finally reached the French border where I was received by French police but this time on a friendly basis.

"The police handed me over to the local authorities and with the help of the French Aero-Club, I was able to contact a German representative in France. He made arrangements for me to travel first to Marseilles, and then by train to Strasbourg and home.

"I reached Germany on 12 February 1938, nearly one year after joining the Legion Condor. After four weeks rest in Kitzbühel, I asked to return to my old unit, JG 132. Then I heard that my *Staffelkapitän*, *Hptm.* Gotthard Handrick (who had achieved fame for his achievements in the 1936 Olympic Games) had been posted to JG 234. I changed my mind and asked to follow him to this unit and my request was accepted. It was with this unit, later known as JG 26, that I would see the beginning of the Second World War."

A low ebb

Following the defeat of the Republicans on the northern front, J/88 withdrew to León for rest and recuperation. On 2 November 1937, a new 4.J/88 was formed under *Oblt.* Eberhard von Trützschler-d'Élsa, its He 51s being shipped from Germany aboard the *Golfo de Panama*. A day earlier the abrasive *Generalmajor* Sperrle was replaced as commander of the Legion Condor by *Generalmajor* Hellmuth Volkmann with *Oberst* Hermann Plocher taking over from von Richthofen as Chief of Staff in January 1938. At this time the Nationalist and Republican Air Forces had approximately the same number of aircraft, but the diversion by the Russians to support the Chinese against the Japanese and the forbidding of the training of further Spanish pilots in French schools did not bode well for the Republicans.

The removal of the threat to the Basque region and Asturia allowed the Nationalists to regroup their forces to concentrate on taking Madrid again. (see map on page 37). Late in November, German and Italian bomber squadrons began carrying out raids on Republican airfields around Madrid, Guadalajara and Bujaraloz in an attempt to neutralise the air threat. The Republican I-15 and I-16 fighters responded to the attacks however, and a number of major air battles took place. Around this time, the I-16 Type 10 had arrived at the front, the new variant being able to out-climb, out-turn and, with its four 7.62 mm machine-guns, out-shoot the Bf 109 B. The Messerschmitt still had a ceiling advantage and was a more stable gun platform. Two major air battles were fought over Alcala de Hanares on 29 and 30 November, pilots from 2.J/88 destroying three *Ratas* on both days.

On 16 December 1937, the Republicans launched a surprise pincer movement, breaking through Nationalist troops and surrounding the exposed town of Teruel. The threat to the town forced 2.J/88 to move to Calamocha airfield to the north and east of Teruel, from where it flew constant ground support operations and escort missions for the bombers of K 88. At this time temperatures were down to as low as -17° C (1.5^{o} F) but some successes were claimed by J/88. Despite these intensive operations, Teruel fell on 8 January 1938.

Generalmajor Hellmuth Volkmann (code named "Vieth"), took over from Sperrle as commander of the Legion Condor in October 1937. He was not particularly popular, constantly pressing for the Legion's withdrawal. He returned to Germany in December 1938, but was killed in a car accident on 21 August 1940 while leading an Infantry Division in France.

Throughout January and almost all of February, Teruel remained the main focus of attention for the Legion Condor. On 18 January, *Oblt.* Wolfgang Schellmann, who had taken over 1.J/88 in December, claimed his first victory, a *Rata*, over Teruel. On the same day, *Lt.* Erich Woitke shot down another I-16, and two days later *Oblt.* Wilhelm Balthasar of 1.J/88 and *Ofw.* Kurt Rochel of 2.J/88 destroyed a *Rata* and a I-15 respectively. Probably the most successful day for J/88 came on 7 February however, when no less than ten SB-2s and two I-16s were destroyed, four of the former falling to the guns of *Lt.* Wilhelm Balthasar within six minutes. Seven further victories were claimed on 21 February, the day that the battered remains of Teruel were finally recaptured by the Nationalists.

On 9 March 1938, Franco decided to change the direction of his assault, advancing east across the Ebro river towards the Mediterranean coast. Again, the Bf 109s of 1. (under *Hptm.* Harro Harder) and 2. (*Oblt.* Joachim Schlichting) J/88 and the He 51s of 3.J/88 under Galland and 4.J/88 under von Trützschler-d'Élsa operated against ground targets. Based at Gallur, they helped the Nationalists to reach the town of Caspe on the Ebro on the 17th. The Bf 109's most successful days during this period came on 10 and 24 March when three Republican aircraft were shot down. But on 30 March, the He 51 piloted by *Hptm.* Hubertus Hering (who was to have succeeded Galland) collided with *Lt.* Manfred Michaelis over Alcarraz, resulting in the death of both pilots.

Early in April, 1. and 2.J/88 transferred from Zaragoza to Lanaja, south of Huesca. During the transfer, on the 4th of the month, *Lt.* Fritz Awe, who had scored three victories with the Bf 109 was killed when his aircraft was struck by that piloted by *Uffz.* Adolf Borchers. Borchers' aircraft also crashed but he escaped with slight injuries. Next day, *Uffz.* Andreas Hester of 4.J/88 was killed when his He 51 was shot down by *Flak*, and seven days later *Uffz.* Gerstmann's aircraft was shot down but he survived with a broken collarbone. On 15 April, Nationalist troops reached the Mediterranean Coast at Vinaroz between Tarragon and Valencia, effectively cutting Republican Spain into two and isolating Barcelona.

Many pilots from our unit "abruptly disappeared..."

EDUARD NEUMANN

"I was born in 1911 in Austro-Hungaria, in an area which was later seeded to Romania. My soldier father was killed in 1914, and my mother died the same year, so I was brought up by my grandparents. I moved to Berlin in order to study and quickly became fascinated with aviation. I soon learned to fly, receiving my pilot certificates in 1932. At that time, I took any opportunity to fly, taking part, for example, in oil prospecting and towing advertisements with my aircraft. In 1934 I entered the *Luftwaffe*, which was then known by the cover name of the *"Deutsche Verkehrs Fliegerschule"*.

"I went to Cottbus in order to gain my certificates, but also joined the infantry to become a soldier. In 1935, I was transferred to Schleissheim where I began training as a fighter pilot. Here I met several men who were to become famous in later years such as Trautloft, Schlichting and Lützow, all of whom were already experienced commanders. After three months, I was posted to II./JG 132 *"Richthofen"* at Jüterbog-Damm where my *Kommandeur* was *Major* Raithel and my *Staffelkapitän* was *Hauptmann* von Schönebeck. Adolf Galland was in the *Gruppenstab*. The *Gruppe* had its origins in the *"Reklamestaffel"*, a formation that taught army pilots under the guise of a civilian unit. Officially, their task was to tow advertising banners, but in fact they were training military pilots, their "towed advertisements" being used as artillery targets! Our squadron at Jüterbog was fully operational, flying He 51s.

Pilots of the Legion Condor enjoying a light lunch at La Cenia with a He 45 B reconnaissance aircraft in the background. Second from the left is Oblt. Eduard Neumann (2 victories), fourth from the left is the Gruppenkommandeur of J/88, Hptm. Gotthard Handrick (5 victories) with Oblt. Eberhard von Trützschler-d'Élsa sixth from the left.

"At the end of 1935, I was called back to the infantry at Leipzig in order to receive officer training. I remained there until the autumn of 1936 when I transferred to *Jagdgruppe Bernburg*, being assigned to Schellmann's *Staffel*. At that time I was an *Oberfähnrich* (officer cadet). It was comic and often difficult, because with three other *Oberfähnriche*, we were the *"Jagdlehrer"* (instructors) and had to teach officers (mainly *Leutnante*).

"At that time, many pilots from our unit "abruptly disappeared". They were called to Berlin and we heard nothing more from them. In fact, even if it was not known officially, we all realised that they had been sent to Spain. One day, a Sunday, I was Officer in Service (*Offz. vom Dienst*), when I received an order to pack immediately and come to Berlin. I was alone. I went directly to the Ministry. The most important thing for them was that I would have no time to speak with anyone else about this call. I was then informed that I would be sent to Spain. I received orders to dress in civilian clothes, and was flown immediately to Rome in a Ju 52 with five other men that I had not previously met, probably technicians. From Rome, we flew to Sevilla.

"Next morning, after my arrival in Sevilla, I was transferred to northern Spain where *Jagdgruppe 88* was based. I met my *Kommandeur*, Handrick and was posted to the *3. Staffel* under the command of Adolf Galland. Amongst my comrades were the future fighter aces, Ewald and Schlichting. The second *Staffel*, under Lützow, was already equipped with Me 109s. We still flew He 51s. During my first operational flight over Asturia, on 4th September 1937, I was flying behind Galland when I sighted a Polikarpov I-15, and I shot it down. It was very hard to do that with a He 51, and it was the first claim of my *Staffel*. In the spring of 1938, Mölders succeeded Galland in command of the *3. Staffel*, and shortly afterwards, I was posted to the *Stab* of J/88, where I often flew as Handrick's wingman. On 10 June 1938, I scored my second victory, a Polikarpov I-16. This gave me the same score as my *Kommandeur*.

"I remained in Spain for one year, moving back to Bad Aibling in South Germany in the summer of 1938. I was happy to see that I had received a large sum of money for my service in Spain. The complete *Staffel* at Bad Aibling, (under *Oberleutnant* Erich Gerlitz) was composed of Austrian pilots. Although I was officially German from 1934, I still remembered my Austrian origins, and was happily accepted by the unit.

LEFT: Hptm. Wolfgang Schellmann caught by the camera during a break from operations. Schellmann, who led 1.J/88, was the second highest German fighter pilot in Spain with twelve victories.

On 23 April, a relatively weak Nationalist force swung southwards, advancing on Valencia. Because of bad weather and a lack of supplies from Germany, which was then engaged in the entry into Austria, the advance was very slow and it was not until July that Nationalist troops neared the city. Sometime earlier, five of the new Bf 109 Cs had been delivered to the *Gruppe* which had now transferred to La Cenia. The new sub-type was powered by the Jumo 210 Ga engine with fuel injection and had an armament of four 7.9 mm machine-guns.

On 18 May 1938, the commander of J/88, *Hptm.* Gotthard Handrick, claimed his only victory in Spain when he shot down an I-16. Three other I-16s were claimed in a massive air battle by pilots of the *2. Staffel.* Flying with them was *Hptm.* Harro Harder who had recently returned for his second tour of duty in Spain. With him he brought the twin 20 mm cannon armed He 112 V9. Six days later *Oblt.* Werner Mölders took over command of 3.J/88 from Galland which was still flying ground support operations with the He 51. Mölders led his first operation against a heavily defended ground target on 31 May, but the aircraft piloted by *Lt.* Fritz Losigkeit was hit by *Flak* and he was forced to bale out. He came down in no-man's land and was captured by Republican forces. Two days later, *Lt.* Haupt was shot down by *Flak*, followed on 8 June by *Lt.* Erich Beyer, both flying He 51s. This led Harder, who was acting commander of the *Jagdgruppe* because Handrick was on leave, to ask for the temporary suspension of operations by 3. and 4.J/88.

The two Bf 109 *Staffeln* continued operations however, five SB-2s being shot down on 2 June with four more Republican aircraft shot down on the 10th. By now the aircraft supply situation was becoming even more serious. Despite often having to fly ten sorties a day, 1.J/88 only had four serviceable Messerschmitts and 2.J/88 seven. Towards the end of June, however, the first of a batch of the new Bf 109 Ds arrived, allowing 3.J/88 to re-equip with the type and bolster the forces of the other two *Staffeln*. At the same time, 4.J/88 was disbanded, its remaining He 51s being passed to the Nationalists.

BELOW: Probably taken at the time Galland handed over command of 3.J/88 to Mölders, this photo shows (from left to right): Ogfr. Iskra (a technician with the Staffel), third from left, Lt. Günther Scholz (one victory in Spain and later Kommodore of JG 5), Lt. Fritz Losigkeit (later Kommodore of JG 77), Hptm. Werner Mölders (with back to camera, 14 victories, later Kommodore of JG 51), Oblt. Adolf Galland (later Kommodore of JG 26) and one of the mechanics.

We flew three to four ground support missions a day at very low level...

ECKEHART PRIEBE

Eckehart Priebe entered the navy as a *"Göring Kadett"* in 1934 and was transferred to the *Luftwaffe* in 1935. He underwent training at the Flying Schools in Ludwigslust and Fassberg and was transferred, during the summer of 1936, to JG 134 *"Horst Wessel"* in Köln. He then served with 1.J/88 in Spain during 1937 and 1938 where he claimed an I-16 *Rata* on 14 May 1938. Up until September 1939, he was General Milch's Adjutant and following the Polish campaign he became *Staffelkapitän* of 2./JG 77. He claimed one victory on 11 October 1939. In May 1940, he claimed two further victories, a Morane 406 on 15th and a Hurricane on the 19th. He was taken prisoner on 31 August 1940 after his Bf 109 E-1 crashed following combat with RAF fighters.

"I was one of the first 186 cadets of the still-secret *Luftwaffe*, soon to be nicknamed *"Göring Kadetten"*. I was the youngest of them all. We were sent to various training units and finally I was transferred to a newly formed fighter *Gruppe* in Köln where I received excellent training by experienced teachers, some of whom had received their training in Soviet Russia under a little-known secret agreement between the Weimar Republic and Moscow. When I received my commission in April 1936, I was also the youngest *Leutnant* in the new *Luftwaffe.*

"The golden days at Köln came to abrupt end when, in the autumn of 1937, I was called to the C.O.'s office who told me under conditions of great secrecy what everyone was hoping for: *"You will report immediately to* Übung Rügen *in Berlin." Übung Rügen* was the code name for the *Legion Condor*, Germany's support of General Franco's fight against Communism in Spain. Our relatives and friends we were told they could write to us from now on via *Max Winkler, Berlin W 8, Postfach 88. "But don't tell them anything else"* we were instructed, *"you are supposed to be in Rügen, a well known island in the Baltic, for manoeuvres."*

"Having received civilian suits from *"Max Winkler"* we set out by freighter from Hamburg with a complete fighter squadron on board - ground staff, pilots, and Heinkel 51s in crates - our destination Vigo on the north-west Spanish coast. We had to dodge the "non-intervention fleet" which was established around the Iberian Peninsular by the League of Nations in an attempt to prevent foreign countries from transporting men and material to the combatants. These where known on one side as "Republicans" and "Rebels" and by the other as "Reds" and "Nationalists". Whenever a boat came into sight, the boatswain would blow the whistle for everybody to hide down below as so many people on the deck of the freighter would have aroused suspicion.

"Once off Vigo, a Nationalist gunboat appeared out of nowhere, claimed us as a war prize and escorted us safely to port where the trains were waiting to take us to León. This was the main base for J/88 as the fighter component of the *Legion Condor* was known. It consisted of two squadrons equipped with Messerschmitt Bf 109 Bs and one with He 51s. Our Heinkels were to form a second He 51 squadron because the older-type biplanes had proved very successful in the ground-attack role.

"We received Spanish uniforms, put our Heinkels together, and off we went to the Guadalajara Mountains for another of those "final assaults on Madrid" which never took place. Instead, on Christmas Eve 1937, we had to hurry to a field called Calamacha, south of Zaragoza, to help the beleaguered garrison at the city of Teruel which the Reds had surrounded in a surprise offensive. For more than two months we were engaged in a most bitter battle in ice-cold Aragonia. It turned out to be a very decisive battle as, after Teruel was recaptured, the Nationalist troops advanced to the Mediterranean, splitting Red-territory in two - the beginning of the end. We flew three to four ground support missions a day at very low level, strafing trenches or dropping our six10 kg bombs on gun positions or military transport. Aerial combat was left to the Bf 109s as the Heinkels were no match for the Soviet-made *Ratas,* the forerunners of the MiGs.

"One day in February 1938, I knocked out a Russian tank by dropping all my bombs in one go. The tank had tried to escape from the encircled city of Teruel. A second tank escaped, swinging around the wreck of the first. We later learned from captured papers that this second tank had carried the Red commander *"El Campesino"* to safety. More than fifty years later after the breakup of the Soviet Union, a Ukranian historian from Odessa asked me to tell him something about the German participation in Spain, anything that might be of interest. Believe it or not, the historian confirmed my story about the escape of *"El Campesino"* and sent me a copy of a Russian newspaper "missing in action" page. This included the name and photo of the tank commander who did not make it: Vladimir Krouchinin.

"After Teruel our squadron re-equipped with the Bf 109 D. In June, I scored my first aerial victory, shooting down a Rata near the city of Sagunto. Some weeks later, it was my turn. I was shot through the lungs in a dogfight and just managed to reach our lines for a landing in some fields before I conked out. The bullet had to be removed in our *Feldlazarett* (Field Hospital) in Zaragoza and I was ordered home for further treatment in a spa in the Black Forest.

"That was the end of a great adventure - over 100 combat missions in a foreign country. I enjoyed the victory parade through the Brandenburg Gate in my hometown of Berlin, a premature promotion to *Oberleutnant*, a bunch of German and Spanish decorations and last, but not least, a lot of money! In addition to our regular pay, we had received 1,200 *Reichsmarks* a month which was not taxed. That paid for a splendid sports car and a lot of fun.

"Many historians have credited the *Legion Condor* with a decisive contribution to the victory of the Nationalist forces. Measured by aerial victories, this might have been true. On the Republican side Spain gained 85, Russia 112, France 20, Bulgaria 22 and America 2 (Frank Tinker and Albert Baeumler). On the Nationalist side Germany gained 314, Spain 176, Italy 72. Many foreign volunteers on the Republican side only realised much later that they were fighting for a Communist dominated regime."

RIGHT: Three Arado Ar 68 Es were delivered to the Legion Condor at La Cenia airfield during the summer 1938. The aircraft is shown just after delivery and no markings have as yet been applied.

LEFT AND BELOW: A total of three Ar 68 E-1s were tested in the night fighter role at La Cenia airfield during the 1937 and 1938. Note that the wheels spats have been removed from 9●1 in the forground. The Luftwaffe also tried using the Ar 68 as an interim night fighter during the late thirties, but without any blind flying aids, the type was not very successful in this role.

Arado Ar 68 E-1

Operated as an interim night fighter from La Cenia airfield, 1937/38. Three Ar 68 Es were used by the Legion Condor and Grupo G-9 of the Nationalist Air Force to operate twilight night fighting sorties, but lacking the proper instrumentation they were not particularly successful.

LEFT: This in flight photo shows the third Ar 68, coded 9●3, of Jagdgruppe 88 which undertook experimental night fighter operations over Castellon. According to one source, the unit that operated them was known as 5.J/88 although this designation is attributed to a unit which operated the Ju 87 dive bomber for a short time.

RIGHT: This in flight shot of a He 51 B-1 with auxiliary tank shows the aircraft with modified markings comprising two black circles under each wing. The Nationalist air forces constantly experimented with national insignia in an attempt to make them as different from those of the Republicans as possible.

BELOW: Front view of a He 51 fighter taxiing to its dispersal. Although the type proved outclassed as a fighter in Spain, it helped develop the ground attack tactics that were adopted during the early years of the Second World War.

LEFT: The He 112 V9, coded 8●2, which was flown by Oblt. Harro Harder during his second tour of duty in Spain. The code prefix "8" was usually carried by captured Polikarpov I-15s, "5" normally being allocated to the He 112. A total of sixteen pre-production He 112 B-0s were delivered to Spain, but these were all flown by Spanish pilots.

BELOW: A mechanic at work on the He 112 V9, the second B-series prototype of the Heinkel fighter. It was powered by a twelve cylinder Jumo 210 Ea engine and carried an armament of two 20 mm MG FF cannon in the wings and two 7.9 mm MG 17 machine-guns in the fuselage nose sychronised to fire through the propeller. The aircraft is shown here before any code numbers were applied.

Heinkel He 112 V9

Flown by Oblt. Harro Harder April 1938 with J/88, this was one of only two He 112s (the V3 and V9) operated by the Legion Condor and the only one to use the code "8". All other He 112s, including those operated by the Spanish Nationalists, carried the code "5". The variation of the swastika emblem was also carried on at least one other aircraft, a He 51, flown by Harder.

LEFT: The Heinkel He 112 V9 was tested by Harro Harder in Spain. The V9 was the second B-series prototype, powered by a 680 hp Jumo 210 Ea engine which gave it a maximum speed of 510 km/h (317 mph) at 4,000 m (13,000 ft). The aircraft originally received the German civil registration D-IGSI but was coded 8●2 in Spain.

ABOVE: A line-up of He 112 B-0s of the Spanish Air Force. The emblem on the tailfin is that of the Patrulla Azul or Blue Patrol.

RIGHT: Lt. Karl Ebbighausen (with his back to the camera) talks to Lt. Günther Scholz in Spain. These two pilots would serve in the Second World War, Ebbighausen as Gruppenkommandeur of II./JG 26 and Scholz as Kommodore of JG 5.

RIGHT: Two He 112 B-0s of the Spanish Grupo 5-G-5 photographed shortly after arrival at León airfield. Note the differing colours of the spinners on these two aircraft.

BELOW: A total of sixteen He 112 B-0s were sent to Spain, coded 5●52 to 5●67, this photograph showing a line-up of five of them. Apart from the V3 and V9 prototypes all the other He 112s were delivered to the Spanish Air Force's Grupo 5-G-5. This unit had the Falangist "Yoke and Arrows" insignia painted in white on their black national insignia circles.

RIGHT: The four Staffelkapitäne of Jagdgruppe 88 photographed in April 1938. From left to right are: Oblt. Wolfgang Schellmann (1.J/88), Oblt. Adolf Galland (3.J/88), Oblt. Joachim Schlichting (2.J/88) and Oblt. Eberhard von Trützschler-d'Élsa (4.J/88).

Heinkel He 51 B-1
Flown by Oberleutnant Adolf Galland of 3.J/88, spring 1938. At this time Galland was Staffelkapitän of 3. J/88. His aircraft had an unusual version of the black fuselage circle which was also overpainted with a Paté style cross. Camouflage was unusual for aircraft in Spain, comprising black-green (70) and dark-green (71) uppersurfaces with pale blue (65)beneath.

The "Mickey Mouse" emblem carried on Galland's He 51.

Three photos of the He 51, coded 2●78, piloted by Oblt. Adolf Galland, Staffelkapitän of 3.J/88. His aircraft carried an unusual Maltese or Paté style cross in white superimposed on the black circle fuselage insignia. The camouflage adopted was similar to that used by contemporary Luftwaffe fighters.

LEFT AND BELOW: On 5 December 1937, Stabsarzt. Dr. Heinrich Neumann crashed this He 51, coded 2●85 while attempting a landing at El Burgo in gusty conditions. This incident led to a ban on further flying of combat aircraft by non-qualified pilots.

ABOVE: Dr. Heinrich Neumann was one of the Legion Condor's medical officers. An amateur pilot, Neumann often used to fly to the various airfields where his patients were based, but this practice came to an end when he crashed a He 51 on 5 December 1937.

Front view of the nose of Heinrich Neumann's He 51 showing the emblem painted on the nose. Unfortunately the details of this are unknown.

RIGHT: **Detail of the upper and lower wing surfaces showing the unusual type of national insignia. It appears that the port aileron had been replaced at some time.**

Heinkel He 51 B-1

Flown by Stabsartz. Dr. Heinrich Neumann, 5 December 1937. Neumann, a doctor of medicine serving with San/88, flew this aircraft unofficially, but on 5 December 1937 crashed it on landing at El Burgo and was badly damaged.

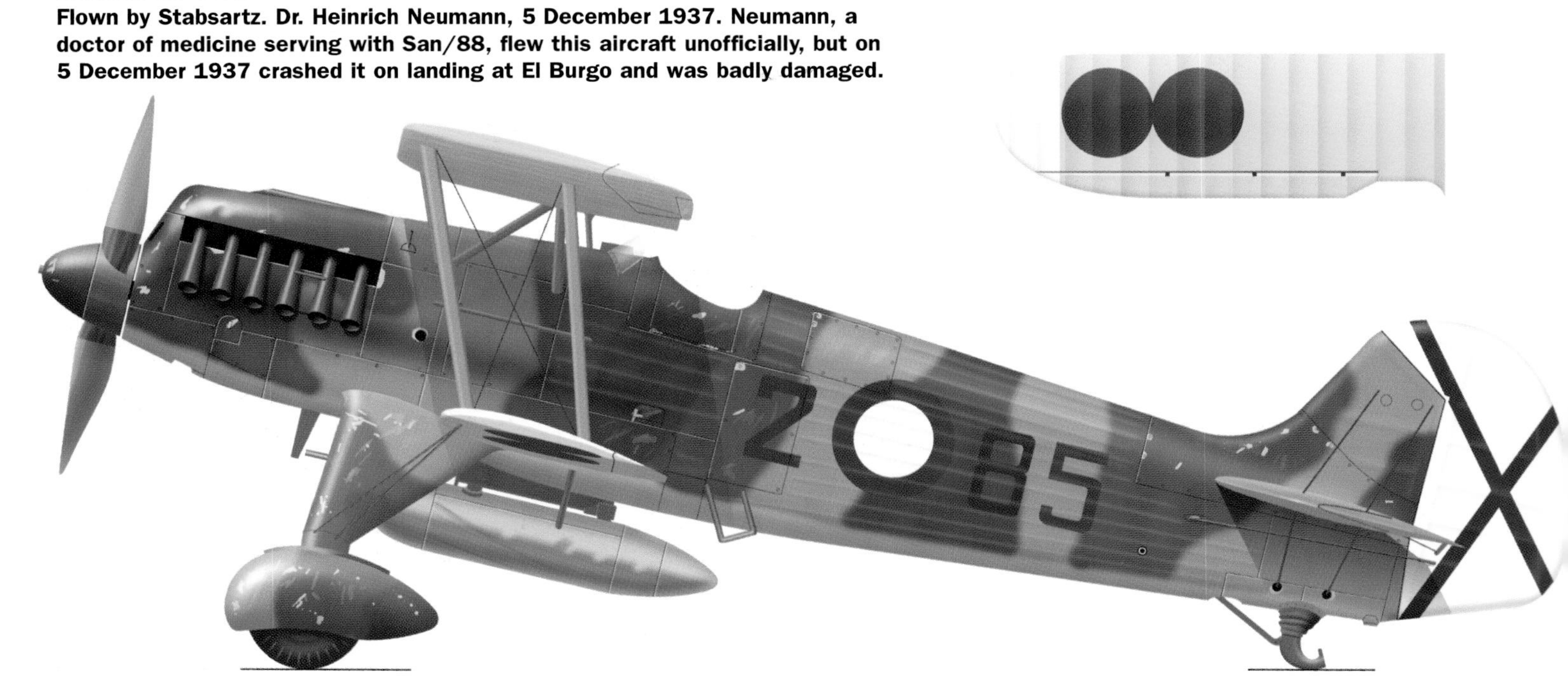

Heinkel He 51 B-1

Flown by Lt. Kurt Strümpell of 3.J/88, February 1938, (not to be confused with his brother, Hennig Strümpell). This aircraft carried a personal black and white insignia, similar to the ancient Chinese "Yin-Yang" symbol, on the fuselage side.

LEFT: Oblt. Hans Schmoller-Haldy (left) and Oblt. Helmut-Felix Bolz of 3.J/88 photographed at Sanjurjo/Zaragoza airfield or in La Cenia in May 1938.

RIGHT: Several He 51s of 1.Staffel of J/88 showing, at the extreme left of the picture, the aircraft, coded 2●98 of Lt. Kurt Strümpell.

BELOW: Lt. Kurt Strümpell of 3.J/88 leaning on the fuselage of his He 51 coded 2●98. His aircraft carried an emblem similar to the ancient Chinese "Yin Yang" symbol for eternity, painted in white on top of the black fuselage circle.

November 1937-June 1938

LEFT: This photograph gives an excellent view of the large white diagonal crosses and white tips painted on the wings of this He 51 in Spain. Most early He 51s were finished in overall pale grey, but when the aircraft was switched to the ground attack role, a wide variety of camouflage schemes were adopted.

BELOW: The front of the engine cowling of the He 51 was a favourite place for the painting of various insignia. This aircraft has the "Totenkopf" (death's head or skull and crossbones) painted in white on dark green camouflage. Note the white tip to the spinner and the markings on the manufacturer's logo on the propeller blades.

ABOVE: When the He 51 was re-assigned to ground attack duties, experiments were conducted to provide a suitable anti-personnel weapon. A simple but effective solution was found by attaching two 10 kg (22 lb) fragmentation bombs to the fuselage drop tank, containing 87 octane aviation fuel, which when dropped, burst open and was ignited by the exploding bombs.

RIGHT: To prevent the He 51 from being blown around in the wind, the aircraft was often weighed down with heavy objects such as bombs (presumably concrete practice weapons or at least unfused!) shown here. The aircraft in the background is a He 111 bomber.

LEFT: A trio of He 51 B-1s in flight. These aircraft carried dark green camouflage patches over their pale grey finish to assist in their role of ground support. The machine nearest the camera, 2●63, has a white cross painted on the front of its engine cowling.

RIGHT: Three main variants of the He 51 were produced, the A, B and C. The He 51 B differed from the A in having twin wire undercarriage bracing and provision for a 170 litre (37.4 Imp gallon) drop tank beneath the fuselage. The He 51 C was factory-fitted with underwing racks for six 10 kg (22 lb) bombs

LEFT: This Legion Condor He 51 B-1 carries a modified version of the black circle national insignia with a white circle superimposed within it similar to that applied to Dr. Neumann's aircraft (see page 144). Like most He 51s in Spain the aircraft has white wingtips.

BELOW: A group of He 51 ground attack aircraft ready for action photographed on a Spanish airfield during the summer of 1938.

ABOVE: Photographed at León airfield in Spain on 24 January 1938 is, at left, a line up of He 51s, with the nose of a He 45 Pavo reconnaissance aircraft at right. The aircraft in the background is probably a captured Vultee V-1A transport.

LEFT: A mechanic sitting on the port wing of a He 51 of 4.J/88 with the "Pik-As" badge painted on the black circle fuselage national insignia. Like many German aircraft in Spain, the He 51 did not carry radio equipment.

ABOVE: A group of pilots gathered around a He 51 of the 4.Staffel of J/88 at Calamocha. The tall figure on the left is Oblt. Eberhard von Trützschler-d'Élsa, Kapitän of 4.J/88 with, in the centre facing the camera: Lt. Heinrich Torner (killed on 19 February 1938), Lt. Fritz Awe (killed on 4 April 1938) and, first from right, Lt. Kurt Müller (3 victories).

LEFT: A total of 126 He 51s were sent to Spain, numbered 2●1 to 2●131, although a few of these codes were not used. The "Pik-As" (Ace of Spades) insignia of 4./J88 will later reused during the Second World War by Jagdgeschwader 53, the "Pik - As Geschwader.

ABOVE: The "second" fourth Staffel of J/88 was formed early in November 1937 under Oblt. Eberhard von Trützschler-d'Élsa for ground attack duties with the He 51. The original 4.J/88 had been disbanded in March 1937.

ABOVE: The headquarters of 3. and 4.J/88 at Darocha showing the badge of both units. This photo was probably taken sometime in November 1937 just after the formation of the second 4.Staffel.

Heinkel He 51 B-1

Flown by Lt. Helmut Henz of 4.J/88, Calamocha, January 1938. This aircraft had a very patchy camouflage most probably applied with a rough brush or even a rag.

BELOW: A line-up of He 51 B-1s photographed at Calamocha airfield in January 1938. The aircraft in the foreground is 2●73 with 2●70 behind. This aircraft was flown by Lt. Helmut Henz of 4.J/88 who was taken prisoner on 14 June 1938 after his He 51 was shot up by a Rata south of Castellon. Note the auxilliary tanks and the personal white script marking under the cockpit of the aircraft in the foreground.

ABOVE: A He 51, coded 2●106, of 4.J/88 based at Darocha airfield during Nationalist operations on the Teruel front. Note the white 'X' on the wings as well as the white wingtips and twin black circles. It is thought that these were introduced to avoid confusion with the Republican roundel marking.

ABOVE: A pair of Bf 109 B-2s in service with Jagdgruppe 88 during the autumn of 1937. The first Messerschmitts were delivered in overall pale grey (63) finish but later this was overpainted with irregular medium green (62) stripes, with the undersides painted in pale blue (65).

ABOVE: A Bf 109 of the 1.Staffel of J/88 carrying seven "kill" markings. This photo shows to advantage the white diagonal cross on a black circle national insignia applied to most aircraft fighting on behalf of the Nationalists in Spain.

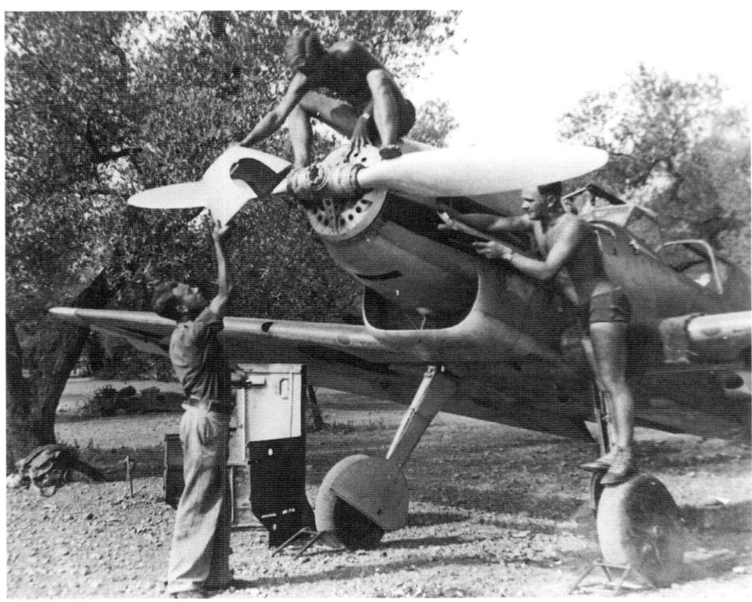

A series of photos showing routine servicing being performed on one of J/88's Bf 109 B-2s. The type was powered by a 600 hp Jumo 210 twelve-cylinder liquid-cooled in-line engine which gave it a maximum speed of 465 km/h (298 mph). The variant also differed from the B-1 in carrying a third 7.9 mm MG 17 machine-gun mounted between the engine cylinder banks, firing through the propeller hub. The first Messerschmitts that went to Spain were not equipped with radio equipment although this became standard in later variants.

ABOVE: This Bf 109 B-2 was flown by Oblt. Walter Oesau who led the Stabskette of J/88. Oesau scored nine victories in Spain before returning to Germany to command III./JG 51, III./JG 3, JG 2 and finally JG 1. The spinner of his aircraft had a small shield painted on one side.

MIDDLE LEFT: A combination of an oxygen cylinder and a stone being used to tether a Bf 109 to the ground in Spain and prevent if from being damaged by wind.
ABOVE: The nose of Oblt. Walter Oesau's Bf 109 D-1 with a black and white shield emblem painted on the spinner. Oesau was to become one of the Luftwaffe's most successful pilots and after his death in 1944, Jagdgeschwader 1 was named after him. At the time this photo was taken, Oesau had eight victories in Spain.
LEFT: The white diagonal cross on a black circle was painted above and below the wings of Spanish Bf 109s, together with white wing tips.

LEFT: This Bf 109 B-2, coded 6●29, taxies towards its take-off point prior to an operation in Spain. The B-2 carried an extra 7.9 mm MG 17 machine-gun firing through the spinner and a VDM metal variable pitch propeller based on American Hamilton patents. Several B-1s were retrospectively modified to use this propeller.

Messerschmitt Bf 109 B-2

Flown by Oblt. Erich Woitke of 1.J/88, February 1938. Like other Bf 109 Bs of the period, this aircraft had medium green patches over its pale grey uppersurfaces with pale blue (65) beneath. The white diagonal cross painted on the black Nationalist black circle marking, was carried by several aircraft from the 1.Staffel. Woitke's aircraft has four victory bars painted on the fin, the last of these, a Rata, being shot down on 21 February 1938.

RIGHT: The Bf 109 B-2 flown by Oblt. Erich Woitke of 1.J/88 photographed in February 1938 at Alfamén airfield on the Belchite front. In this photo the uppersurfaces of the aircraft appear to be one colour, but other photos show it to have patches of grey and green as shown in the colour drawing. Woitke was killed in action as Gruppenkommandeur of III./JG 1 on 24 December 1944.

LEFT: A newly arrived German "volunteer" still in civilian clothes examines a Bf 109 B-2 of Jagdgruppe 88 in Spain. Operational Nationalist aircraft were all given an aircraft identification number. Numbers from 1 to 9 were fighters, 10 to 19 were reconnaissance aircraft, 20 to 29 were bombers, 30 to 39 were light aircraft and 40 to 49 were transports.

BELOW LEFT AND RIGHT:
A pair of photos showing a crane truck being used to assist in changing an engine on the Bf 109. The 1,100 hp Daimler-Benz DB 601 A twelve cylinder liquid-cooled in-line engine which powered the Bf 109 E series weighed around 600 kg (1300 lbs), but was relatively easy to replace. After being removed, the old engine was stored on the back of the truck for transport to a maintenance facility.

The Bf 109 B-2 could be distinguished from the B-1 by its Hamilton metal variable pitch propeller, the earlier variant having a wooden unit. A total of four prototype, forty-one B-series, five C-series, thirty-six D-series and forty-five E-series Bf 109s were sent to Spain - 131 aircraft in all.

RIGHT: This Bf 109 B-2, photographed during the autumn of 1937, was normally flown by Uffz. Ernst Terry. The aircraft was later transferred to the Spanish 5-G-5 Group.

The second Messerschmitt Bf 109 C-1
Only five Bf 109 C-1s were delivered to Spain during the spring of 1938. The variant was powered by a 700 hp Jumo 210 G engine with direct fuel injection which gave it a maximum speed of 465 km/h (289 mph). Armament was also increased to four 7.9 mm MG 17 machine-guns.

RIGHT: Although of poor quality, this is one of only two known photographs of a Bf 109 C-1 in Spain. Powered by a fuel injected Jumo 210 G engine, the aircraft carried an armament of four 7.9 mm MG 17 machine-guns, two in the wings and two in the fuselage. Only five Bf 109 Cs were sent to Spain, numbered 6●46 to 6●50.

LEFT: This Bf 109 B-2, coded 6●36, was flown by Hptm. Harro Harder, Staffelkapitän of 1.J/88 during the autumn of 1937. The white diagonal cross marking was a variant of the swastika insignia used earlier by Harder. It was later used by the whole of the first Staffel.

LEFT: The fourth Bf 109 C-1 sent to Spain was coded 6●49. Relatively few of these aircraft, with fuel injected Jumo 210 G engines, were built.

BELOW: The Fieseler Fi 156 "Ciguana" (better known in Germany as the "Storch"), this one, coded 46●2, was used exclusively as a liaison aircraft by the General Staff of the Legion Condor. This type had only just started to enter service with the Luftwaffe in Germany and several of these machines were sent to Spain for evaluation by the Luftwaffe under operational conditions. The aircraft behind is a Heinkel He 45 biplane which was rapidly becoming obsolete by this time and was probably only used for communication purposes.

ABOVE: The first Fieseler Fi 156, coded 46●1, was extensively damaged when the undercarriage collapsed during a landing in Ávila.

LEFT: Illustrating some of the unusual camouflage schemes applied to the He 51 in Spain, this aircraft was actually flown by Candidate Queipo de Llano, an officer cadet serving with a Spanish unit. In an attempt to distinguish the He 51 from similar Republican aircraft, the He 51s often had two black circles and white diagonal crosses painted on each wing together with white wingtips.

"Marabu" (Marabou) badge

ABOVE: Photographed at Calamocha, this He 51, coded 2●86, was piloted by Uffz. Erich Kuhlmann of 1.J/88. Below the cockpit can be seen the "Marabu" badge carried by the Staffel while equipped with the Heinkel.

RIGHT: Following its transfer to the ground attack role, the He 51 adopted a variety of camouflage finishes. This aircraft, with its auxiliary fuel tank, had large patches of dark green paint over its grey uppersurfaces with pale blue beneath.

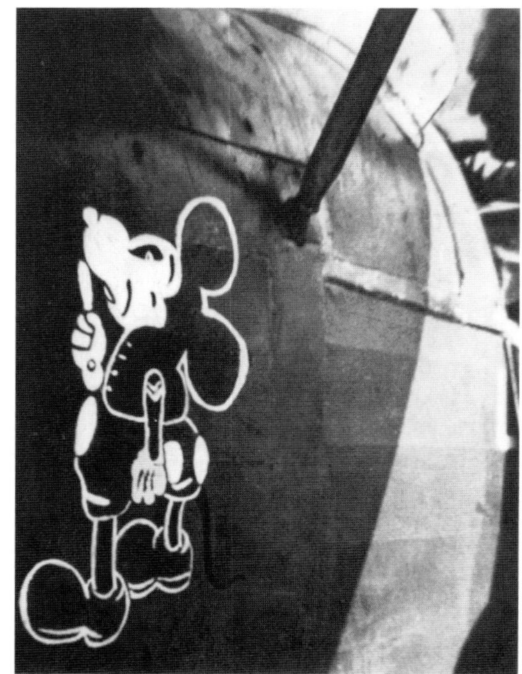

BELOW: Close-up of the Mickey Mouse badge carried by several aircraft of 3.J/88, including those flown by Adolf Galland and Dr. Heinrich Neumann.

ABOVE: Illustrated in colour below, this photo shows the He 51 B-1, coded 2●102 as piloted by Dr. Heinrich Neumann. Below the cockpit can be seen the legend "Annelis" in white, probably the name of his wife or girl friend.

Heinkel He 51 B-1

Flown by Stabsartz. Dr. Heinrich Neumann, early 1938. After Dr. Neumann crashed his earlier Heinkel he was allowed to fly another, this time with official blessing. This machine bears the legend "Tut mir nichts, ich tu' Euch auch nichts!" ("If you don't do anything to me, I won't won't do anything to you!") painted on the side of the fuselage in white.

RIGHT: A newly painted He 51 with what appears to be dark green and pale grey finish. Note the sharp demarcation line between the upper camouflage finish and the pale-blue (65) undersides.

LEFT: He 51, coded 2●28, after a landing mishap, probably due to the starboard undercarriage hitting a pot-hole. Note that the fuel tank has been discharged during the mission. The aircraft probably only has minor damage as the ground towing device, seen in the centre front of the picture, is ready for use for when the aircraft has been righted.

"Mickey Mouse", the popular Walt Disney cartoon character of the time, was painted on many German aircraft including those operating in Spain. The above example was painted as shown on Heinrich Neumann's aircraft shown opposite.

ABOVE AND RIGHT: Apart from Germany, the Spanish Nationalists also received considerable military assistance from Italy. The most numerous Italian fighter to serve in the theatre was the Fiat C.R.32, a biplane powered by a 600 hp Fiat A30 twelve cylinder liquid cooled in-line engine. The aircraft had a maximum speed of 355 km/h (221 mph) at 3,000 m (10,000 ft) and carried an armament of two 12.7 mm Breda-SAFAT heavy machine-guns.

I was very surprised to learn that aerial combat was forbidden...

GÜNTHER SCHOLZ

"On 15 February 1938, I was assigned to 10./JG 137, a unit which only existed on paper. This unit was in fact a smokescreen used to maintain the total secrecy which surrounded the German intervention in the Spanish Civil War. It was commanded by *Oblt*. Jürgen Roth who had already completed a "tour" in Spain as *Staffelkapitän* of 3.J/88 during 1936-37. Our first duty was to be briefed on all aspects of our future conduct in Spain. Then, on 27 March 1938, we left for Berlin and flew to Rome in a Ju 52 transport. There we received money to pay for two day's stay in a hotel, and then we boarded another Ju 52 to Sevilla. At this time there was at least one other aircraft flying with us.

"In Sevilla we were taken by a waiting car to the *Christina* hotel, and the next day we flew to Burgos. Here we received our Legion Condor uniforms and then waited for the *Jagdgruppe's* transport to ferry us to Saragossa-San Jurgo airfield. On our arrival, we "green" pilots were posted to Adolf Galland's third (ground attack) *Staffel*. I was very surprised to learn that aerial combat was forbidden. The fact was that our He 51s were outclassed in the air by the more modern Soviet-built machines which opposed them. In order to avoid losses, our briefing was to only drop bombs or to strafe enemy positions. The Polikarpov *"Ratas"* were lighter and just a little faster which rendered them superior to our fighters until the arrival of the Bf 109. The new fighter was delivered to my unit a little later, although *Oblt*. Günther Lützow's 2.J/88 already had Messerschmitts. We then transferred our He 51s to the Spanish Air Force.

"At this time we used a train to provide us with living accommodation and act as mobile headquarters. This train also carried supplies but it eventually had to be abandoned because of a damaged bridge. Every *Staffel* had its own translator and we were fortunate in gaining the services of *Herr* Löffler (a German national who owned a hotel in Madrid) who helped us with our shopping in the local villages. We had no difficulty in buying anything we wanted as our pay was good; 1,200 *Reichsmarks* (or 4,000 *Pesetas* a month for a *Leutnant*). Half of this amount was paid in *Pesetas*, the remainder being sent to a special account in Germany. We also had an arrangement with a Spanish brothel keeper who brought her "ladies" to our airfield, where they "worked" under the guard of a soldier.

"I had one victory in Spain, a *Rata* shot down on 19 August 1938, J/88's 212th kill. In September 1938, many fighter and bomber pilots were recalled to Germany because of the Sudeten Crisis. We boarded a boat at La Coruña harbour and followed the Atlantic coastline through the Bay of Biscay, the English Channel and eventually to Hamburg. Our boat was registered under the Panamanian flag. If we encountered a British merchant or naval vessel we had to quickly disappear below decks. I left the so-called *"RLM Sonderstab 10"* (a cover name for the Legion Condor) on 10 September and was then posted to I./JG 131 based at Jesau."

This He 51, coded 2●60 of 4./J88, carries the "Pik-As" badge. Several other He 51s can be seen in the background.

The End in Spain

As previously mentioned, bad weather dogged operations in late June and early July 1938, but on 12 July, preparations for an all out offensive against Valencia were completed. A period of great success followed for J/88. It began on the 12th when *Lt.* Wilhelm Keidel and *Fw.* Herbert Ihlefeld each shot down an I-15. Three days later no less than nine *Chatos* were destroyed by pilots of J/88, one of them falling to Mölders, his first victory. On 17 July, six more I-15s were shot down with four *Ratas* following next day and five more on the 19th. Three I-16s and a *Chato* followed on 20 July prompting the Germans to report:

"In the five days since the delivery of 22 new Bf 109s, the German Jagdgruppe *has shot down 22 Red fighters without loss."*[1]

The successes were to continue, J/88 destroying four more Republican aircraft on 23 July. Two days later, Republican troops launched a surprise counter attack across the River Ebro between Mequinenza and Amposta, advancing on Gandesa. Before ground reinforcements could arrive, the Nationalist air forces were thrown against the incursion, J/88 based at La Cenia flying fighter protection for the bombers of K/88. Nevertheless, within three days the Republicans had captured 600 sq km (230 sq mls) of territory and it was not until early August that the situation was stabilised. During the air operations, a SB-2 was shot down on 27 July and four days later three *Chatos* were shot down by 3.J/88, followed by a *Rata* on 2 August. Ten days later, 1.J/88 destroyed three SB-2s and a *Rata*, but next day the unit encountered the I-16 Type 10 (often known as the *"Super Rata"*) for the first time. Another large air battle developed on 14 August with 1. and 3.J/88 shooting down no less than seven *Ratas*.

On 19 August, seven Nationalist divisions counter attacked towards Fatarelle with strong support from the Legion Condor. Although J/88 destroyed four *Ratas* little success was achieved on the ground. Next day, Schellmann scored his twelfth and last victory in Spain, making him the highest scoring German pilot to date. On the ground, Nationalist troops began to make slow inroads into the Republican advance while in the air J/88 destroyed four aircraft on 23 August and five more by the 9 September. One of these was Mölders' sixth victory.

Handrick was finally relieved as commander of *Jagdgruppe 88* on 10 September, his place being taken by *Hptm.* Walter Grabmann who had previously led I./JG 234. Around the same time, *Hptm.* Siebelt Reents took over from Schellmann as *Kapitän* of 1.J/88 and by this time many other experienced pilots had returned to Germany due to the looming Sudeten crisis. Successes continued however, four Republican aircraft being shot down on 20 September, ten on 23rd and four on 27th. On 4 October, two I-15s and an I-16 were destroyed by J/88.

At the end of October, the Nationalists launched a major offensive on the Ebro battlefield. Although still possessing about a hundred fighters, the Republicans could not claim air superiority. Trying to penetrate the Nationalist screen of Bf 109 and Fiat fighters, they lost eight I-16s and two I-15s to the guns of 2. and 3.J/88. On 3 November, Nationalist forces captured the town of Pinell, marking the first major breakthrough at the Ebro. J/88 claimed six more kills, one of them the 14th and last by *Hptm.* Mölders. The Ebro battle continued until 16 November 1938 by which time the Nationalists had regained all the territory lost. The three and a half month battle had resulted in the loss of 300 Republican aircraft, over one third being destroyed by J/88 and no fewer than 42 by Mölders' *3. Staffel.*

After the battle of the Ebro, the Legion Condor was ordered to rest with only one *Staffel* of J/88 remaining operational. At the end of November, Volkmann was replaced by von Richthofen as commander of the Legion, with *Obstlt.* Hans Seidemann

Generalmajor Hellmuth Volkmann (left), the second head of the Legion Condor, with General Alfredo Kindelan y Duany, the head of the Spanish Nationalist Air Force. Kindelan was often heard to remark that the Nationalists could get along well without the Legion Condor.

Heinkel He 51 C-1 of 4.J/88
Based at Calamocha, spring 1938, this aircraft has a variation of the dark brown (61), medium green (62) and pale grey (63) uppersurfaces with pale blue (65) beneath. The "Pik-As" (Ace of Spades) insignia was carried by the second 4.J/88 which was formed on 2 November 1937.

LEFT: This He 51, coded 2●106, of 4.J/88 is under guard by the Spanish "Guardia Civil". The "Pik-As" emblem was introduced at the beginning of November 1937 by Oblt. Eberhard von Trützschler-d'Élsa when he formed the second 4.Staffel. The original 4.J/88 which had been formed from the first group of fighter pilots which went to Spain in August 1936, was disbanded in March 37. A total of 126 He 51s were sent to Legion Condor, numbered 2●1 to 2●131 although some of these codes were not used.

RIGHT: When the second 4.J/88 was formed on 2 November 1937, the unit adopted a "Pik-As" (ace of spades) badge for its He 51s. This badge was later adopted by JG 53 (formed from JG 334 by way of JG 133) which became known as the "Pik-As Geschwader".

taking over from Plocher as chief of staff. Mölders also left Spain at this time, his place as commander of 3.J/88 being taken by *Oblt.* Hubertus von Bonin.

On 23 December, the Nationalists launched what was to be the last major offensive in which the Legion Condor was involved. The plan was to strike north and east with the intention of taking Barcelona and the area bordering France. By this time the first Bf 109 E-1s were delivered to J/88 at La Cenia, the new variant being powered by a 1,100 hp Daimler-Benz 601A engine which gave a maximum speed of around 555 km/h (345 mph). Between 28 and 30 December, J/88 shot down 16 Republican aircraft including one by *Oblt.* Alfred von Lojewski, the new commander of the *2. Staffel.*

Bad weather was to curtail operations during this period, but on 12 January 1939, Bf 109s of J/88 carried out a surprise attack on Republican airfields, destroying 13 aircraft on the ground. As the Nationalists continued to advance on Barcelona, 3.J/88 shot down four aircraft on 17 January and four days later the *Gruppe* moved to Valls airfield north of Tarragona. Barcelona fell on 26 January and two days later the Bf 109s from J/88 guarded a large victory parade over the city in case there should be a surprise attack. The next few days were spent in pursuing what remained of the Republican forces towards the Pyrenees, but heavy rainstorms restricted operations on 30 January. Early in February, J/88 flew escort missions and attacks on Republican airfields,shooting down three aircraft on 5 February and four on the 6th. On this day, the unit suffered its last operational loss when *Uffz.* Heinrich Windemuth's Bf 109 E-1, coded 6-89, crashed in flames during an attack on Vilajuiga airfield. On 6 March, J/88 scored its 314th and last victory, a "Curtiss" shot down by *Oblt.* Hubertus von Bonin of the *3. Staffel.*

The Legion Condor took little part in the final offensive against Madrid, flying what were described as "practice missions" during the final days of the war. J/88 flew an operation on 17 March when several Bf 109s carried out a *"freie Jagd"* over Madrid but without meeting any opposition. The last sortie came on 27 March when the unit escorted the bombers of K/88 for a final mission against forward Republican positions. Early the same day a Hs 126 reconnaissance aircraft reported seeing white flags flying in the capital, and at 10.00 am von Richthofen sent the long-awaited message to his squadrons: "All German units will cease operations!"

The support of Germany and Italy for the Nationalists, and the Soviet Union for the Republicans had turned what began as a ill-fated *coup d'état* into a long and bloody civil war. Though German aid to Franco never equalled that given by Italy, the Germans estimated that they had spent half a billion *Reichsmarks* on the venture. In addition they had tested aircraft, tanks and tactics which were to prove invaluable during the Second World War.

---

1. German Situation Report No.541 of 20 July, 1938.

Possibly taken after Wolfram von Richthofen returned to Spain in December 1938, this photo shows a group of men talking to the General with a Junkers Ju 52/3m transport in German civil markings in the background.

BELOW: The three highest scoring German fighter pilots in Spain share a joke. From left is Hptm. Wolfgang Schellmann, who led 1.J/88 and scored 12 victories, Hptm. Harro Harder, who led 1.J/88 before Schellmann and had 11 victories and Hptm. Werner Mölders, who led 3.J/88 and scored 14 victories.

ABOVE: A group of Spanish and Moroccan troops seated in front of a He 51 undergoing routine maintenance. The aircraft carries a figure "7" in the typically Germanic style.

ABOVE AND LEFT: This Bf 109 "Bipala", coded 6●51 was the first D-1 to be delivered to Spain. The aircraft is seen here after the end of civil war with Spanish Air Force red-yellow-red roundels under the wings.

LEFT AND BELOW: These close ups show the Junkers Jumo 210 Da twelve-cylinder inverted-Vee liquid cooled in-line engine fitted to the Bf 109 D-1. For many years after the war, it was thought that the D-variant was powered by the experimental 1,000 hp Daimler-Benz DB 600 A engine, a result of successful German propaganda.

ABOVE: The third Bf 109 D to be delivered to Spain photographed during the summer of 1938.

LEFT: Undercarriage retraction tests being carried out on a Bf 109 D-1. For this, the aircraft was mounted on hydraulic jacks.

ABOVE: This 109 D-1, coded 6●51 is generally thought to be the aircraft piloted by Hptm. Wolfgang Schellmann who led 1.J/88 from 19 December 1937 to 2 September 1938. He was the second highest German fighter pilot in Spain after Mölders with 12 victories. The aircraft shown here has six kills on the tail which suggests that the photo was taken in mid-1938. Hptm. Harro Harder, the second Staffelkapitän of 1.J/88 adopted the white-diagonal cross superimposed on the black fuselage national insignia.

BELOW: A Schwarm of Bf 109 D-1s from 1.J/88 with 6●51 nearest the camera. This aircraft was probably the mount of Hptm. Wolfgang Schellmann. In this photo his aircraft carries five victories, this, a Rata, being claimed on 25 June 1938. The white diagonal cross emblem was introduced by Hptm. Harro Harder, the second Staffelkapitän of 1.J/88.

Messerschmitt Bf 109 D-1

Flown by Oberleutnant Wolfgang Schellmann, Staffelkapitän of 1.J/88, June 1938. The first Bf 109 D-1 delivered to the Legion Condor, this aircraft had overall medium green (62) uppersurfaces with pale blue (65) beneath. Schellmann had shot down four Republican aircraft at this time, eventually destroying a total of 12 which made him the second highest scoring German pilot in Spain. The next aircraft, coded 6●52, was delivered to 2.J/88.

6●51

Three close-ups showing a Bf 109 D-1 being re-armed. The variant carried an armament of two 7.9 mm MG 17 machine guns above the cowling and two MG 17s in the wings. Note the sideways-hinging canopy which was a feature of the Messerschmitt fighter throughout its life.

July 1938-March 1939

TOP LEFT AND ABOVE: Two views of Gotthard Handrick's Bf 109 D showing the Olympic ring insignia on the spinner. Close-up details of these are given on the opposite page. Most D-series aircraft could be distinguished from the earlier models by the small exhaust ejector stubs.

LEFT: The Kommandeur of J/88, Hptm. Gotthard Handrick (with the stick), relaxes in Spain during the summer of 1938. Appointed Kommodore of JG 26 on 24 June 1940, he was replaced by Adolf Galland after only two months in this position. He survived the war and died in 1978.

LEFT: The Bf 109 D-1 piloted by Hptm. Gotthard Handrick, commander of J/88. Apart from having the Olympic rings painted on the spinner of his aircraft, Handrick also had a white script "h" superimposed on the black fuselage national insignia. After returning to Germany, Handrick took over command of I./JG 234 (later I./JG 26) and later became Geschwaderkommodore.

RIGHT: The Bf 109 D-1 flown by the Kommandeur of J/88. It is difficult to tell whether the pilot at the time this photo was taken was Hptm. Gotthard Handrick or Hptm. Walter Grabmann as neither the white script "h" of the former or the white capital "G" of the latter was applied to the starboard side of the aircraft. Handrick would end the conflict with five victories, Grabmann with seven.

LEFT: One side of the spinner of Hptm. Gotthard Handrick's Bf 109 D-1 was marked with the five Olympic rings to commemorate his winning a Gold Medal in the 1936 Berlin Games together with the legend "1936" and a laurel wreath. This photo was taken after the aircraft had been decorated by his ground crew to commemorate his return to Germany in September 1938. The inscription "Scheiden tut weh" means "Parting is painful".
ABOVE: The other side of the spinner of Handrick's Bf 109 D-1 with the five Olympic rings and the legend "1940?" This recorded Handrick's hope that he would win a second Olympic Gold Medal at the 1940 Games scheduled to take place in Tokyo. The nose of the spinner was painted in concentric red, yellow and red bands.

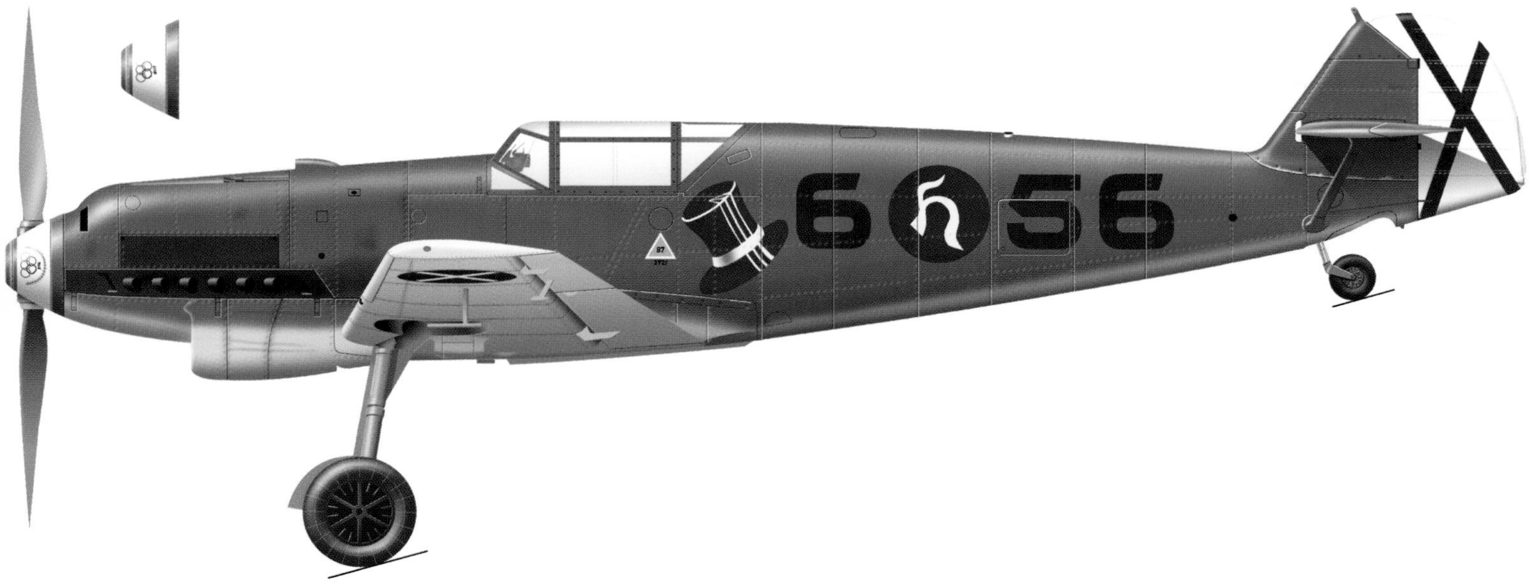

LEFT: A Bf 109 D photographed on a Spanish airfield. A total of 36 D-series aircraft were delivered to the Legion Condor for use by Jagdgruppe 88, numbered 6●51 to 6●86.

ABOVE: After Handrick handed over command of J/88 in September 1938, 6●56 was taken over by the new commander, Hptm. Walter Grabmann who substituted the script "h" with a "G". On his return to Germany, Grabmann took over command of I.(schwere J)/LG 1 and then became Kommodore of ZG 76. He ended the Second World War as a divisional commander. 6●56 was later passed to the Patrulla Azul (Blue Patrol) of the Spanish Air Force, the script "G" then being replaced by a Falangist "Yoke and Arrows" insignia.

BELOW: As indicated above, the Bf 109 D-1 coded 6●56 was eventually passed to the Spanish Patrulla Azul (Blue Patrol). The badge of the unit was painted in blue and white on the aircraft's fin.

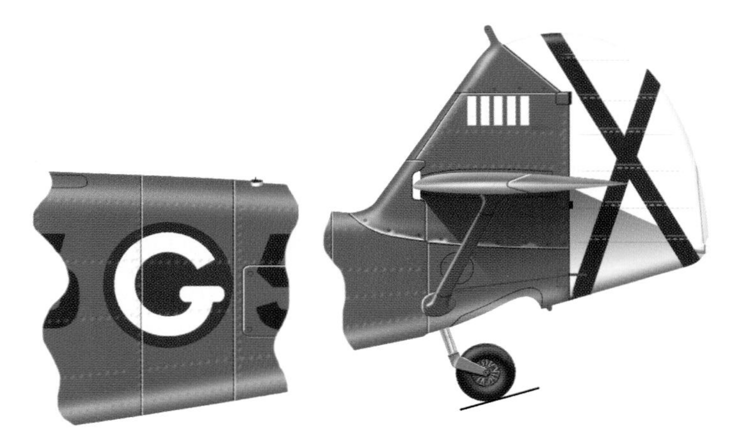

Messerschmitt Bf 109 D-1
In September 1938, the aircraft was taken over by the new commander of J/88, Hptm. Walter Grabmann, who substituted the script "h" with a "G". At the end of the Spanish Civil War, the aircraft was passed to the Patrulla Azul (Blue Patrol) of the Spanish Air Force, the script "G" then being replaced by the Falangist "Yoke and Arrows" insignia.

LEFT: Various forms of Mickey Mouse insignia were carried by aircraft of 3.J/88 in Spain. It would appear that in this instance, Mickey wore red trousers and collar. The emblem was later used by several Luftwaffe units.

ABOVE: Hauptmann Werner Mölders, affectionately known as "Vati" (Daddy) was the highest scoring German fighter pilot in Spain with 14 victories. He developed the tactic of assembling his fighters in a loose formation of four (the Schwarm), tactics which were to stand the Jagdwaffe in good stead during the Battle of Britain.

RIGHT: The Mickey Mouse emblem indicates this Bf 109 D-1 was operated by 3.J/88 but unfortunately the identity of the pilot is unknown. Six white victory bars were painted on the fin.

BELOW: A mechanic poses in front of Hptm. Werner Mölders' Bf 109 D-1, coded 6●79, with the Mickey Mouse emblem introduced for 3.J/88 when it was led by Oblt. Douglas Pitcairn. This photo was taken on 15 July 1938 before his first victory claim, a "Curtiss". After Mölders returned to Germany, his aircraft was allocated by junior pilots to give them confidence.

Details of Mölders' "Mickey Mouse" badge

ABOVE: The rudder of Hptm. Werner Mölders's Bf 109 D-1 showing fifteen white victory bars. It is widely accepted that Mölders claimed fourteen victories in Spain, so this picture remains somewhat of a mystery. Whether he considered one of his victories had not be recognised, or whether one of his mechanics simply anticipated another "kill" is unknown.

Messerschmitt Bf 109 D-1

Flown by Hauptmann Werner Mölders, Staffelkapitän of 3.J/88, November 1938. Mölders' aircraft had medium green (62) uppersurfaces with the name "Luchs" (Lynx) painted on the fuselage side. This may have been applied by his ground crew to indicate that he had eyes like a lynx. Although it is generally accepted that Mölders shot down a total of 14 Republican aircraft in Spain, the rudder of his machine was marked with fifteen victory bars.

Oblt. Werner Mölders talks to one of his mechanics as his aircraft, coded 6●79, is prepared for another operation. Mölders' aircraft had the named "Luchs" (Lynx) painted on both sides of the engine cowling, with the "Mickey Mouse" emblem of 3.J/88 on the port side.

ABOVE: Mölders's wingman, Uffz. Franz "Francisco" Jaenisch, who took over Ihlefeld's Bf 109. He ended the conflict with one victory.

ABOVE: A mechanic working on the last Bf 109 D-1 to be sent to Spain coded 6●86. The aircraft was delivered to 1.J/88 which had just adopted the "Holzauge" emblem.

RIGHT: The aircraft nearest the camera was the first Bf 109 E-1, coded 6●87, to be delivered to Spain. Photographed at Zaidin airfield in December 1938 together with a group of Bf 109 B-2s in the background. The aircraft had medium green uppersurfaces, (similar to RLM colour (62) but possibly a little paler. The undersides were finished in pale blue (65).

Messerschmitt Bf 109 E-1

The first Messerschmitt Bf 109 E-1 to arrive in Spain at Zaidin airfield, December 1938. The E model Bf 109 retained the medium green uppersurface camouflage with pale blue beneath carried by previous variants in Spain. The painting of black patches around the exhaust area was common to Bf 109 Es operating in the Spanish Civil war.

LEFT AND RIGHT: The "Holzauge" (wooden eye) insignia introduced by Hptm. Siebelt Reents, the last Kapitän of 1.J/88. The "Holzauge" was a reference to the Spanish gesture of pulling down the bottom eyelid with one finger to indicate caution.

LEFT: On 2 September 1938. Oblt. Siebelt Reents took over command of 1.J/88 from Wolfganf Schellmann. He introduced the "Holzeuge" emblem which was normally painted on both sides of the fuselage of the unit's Bf 109 Es. However the positioning of where the emblem was painted varied (see page 176) as did the actual artwork.

BELOW: The fourth Bf 109 E-1 to be sent to Spain was 6●90 shown here at Zaragoza just before being handed over to the Spanish Air Force at the end of the Civil War.

BELOW: Oblt. Siebelt Reents' Bf 109 E coded 6●88, stands ready for action in the late afternoon sun, with the mechanics tidying up after completing their task

RIGHT: Three Bf 109s return from a mission with a Bf 109 E-1, coded 6●91 in the foreground.

RIGHT: This Bf 109 E-1, 6●98, was flown by Fw. Heinrich Windemuth who crashed and was killed during a ground attack on Vilajuiga airfield on 6 February 1939. At the time he was credited with having one victory.

BELOW: A group of Bf 109 E-3s after delivery to Spain with 6●101 in the foreground and 6●91 behind. Bf 109s with codes between 6●87 and 6●131 were allocated to E-series aircraft.

BELOW: The Bf 109 E-1 in the background, coded 6●104, was transferred to the Spanish Grupo 5-G-5 at the end of the war in Spain. Both Bf 109 E-1s and E-3s were sent to Spain, the latter differing mainly in having the two 7.9 mm MG 17 machine-guns replaced by two 20 mm MG FF cannon.

ABOVE AND RIGHT: As the conflict drew towards its eventual Nationalist victory, German aircrews found themselves less involved. By the time the Bf 109 Es had become common-place the Republican Airforce had more or less been eliminated. These times gave ample opportunities for flying practice with the new fighter and these photos also show the wide variety of flying uniforms worn by German personnel.

LEFT AND BELOW: Taken at a parade held after the end of the war at Sanjurjo/Zaragoza airfield this line-up of Bf 109 E-3s of Jagdgruppe *88* were eventually handed over to the Spanish Air Force.

LEFT AND BELOW: Ground crews struggle to recover this Bf 109 E, coded 6●107, after the starboard undercarriage leg collapsed. The aircraft has the legend "Mors Mors" painted above the exhaust in white.

Another variation of the "Zylinder hut" (top hat) badge carried by the Bf 109 E, coded 6●107 of 2.J/88.

ABOVE: A group photo of 1.J/88, from left: Uffz. Halupczek, Uffz. Holitzke, Uffz. Nirminger (partly hidden), Oblt. "Fürst" Wilcke, Lt. Roedel, Hptm. Reents (Staffelkapitän), Oblt. von Holtey, Lt. Sandmann, Lt. von Minnigerode, Oblt. Hollweg and Lt. Schumann

ABOVE: A total of 45 Bf 109 Es were delivered to Jagdgruppe 88 in Spain, coded 6●87 to 6●131.

LEFT: This Bf 109 E-3 coded 6●111, which was flown by Lt. Werner Ursinus of 2.J/88, had the name "Bärchen" painted in white below the cockpit. "Ursinus" means "Teddy Bear" in Latin and the German for that toy is "Bärchen". On his return to Germany, Ursinus led 3./JG 53 until the end of August 1941 when he took over the Ergänzungsstaffel of JG 53. He survived the war as an instructor.

Messerschmitt Bf 109 E-3

Flown by Lt. Werner Ursinus of 2.J/88, spring 1939. The name "Bärchen" (Teddy Bear) was painted below the cockpit of his aircraft. "Ursinus" means "Teddy Bear" in Latin, hence the connection. Ursinus did not claim any victories with 2.J/88 in Spain but later went on to serve with JG 53 in France, the Battle of Britain and Russia.

The Bf 109 E-1 was undoubtedly the finest fighter to be used in the Spanish Civil War. By the time it was available in numbers the enemy threat had largely diminished and only few "Emils" saw combat. An unusual feature of many Bf 109 Es in Spain was the painting of large black patches extending from the exhausts to mask any smoke blackening from the engines.

LEFT: The *"Holzauge"* (wooden eye) insignia, this time positioned immediately below the cockpit of a Bf 109 E of 1.J/88.

ABOVE: A Schwarm of four Bf 109 Es of 1.J/88 in flight over Spain with the aircraft flown by the Staffelkapitän, Hptm. Siebelt Reents nearest the camera. When flying operationally, the aircraft would be spread much further apart.

Messerschmitt Bf 109 E-3
Flown by Hptm. Siebelt Reents, Staffelkapitän of 1.J/88, spring 1939. Reents' aircraft had the "Holzauge" (Wooden Eye) badge introduced for aircraft of the 1.Staffel of J/88 at this time.

RIGHT: Illustrated in colour above, this Bf 109 E was flown by Siebelt Reents, Staffelkapitän of 1.J/88. Note the black area painted from the exhaust to behind the wing leading edge designed to hide the smoke blackening from the Daimler-Benz DB 601 engine.

LEFT: A group of Bf 109 Es after being assembled at Leon prior to being handed over to the Spanish Air Force following the end of the war. The machine in the foreground, 6●119 with the "Holzauge" badge, was flown by the last Kapitän of 1.J/88, Hptm. Siebelt Reents while Oblt. Schmoller-Haldy's 6●123 can be seen in the background.

RIGHT: Taken at the same time as the photo at the top left of page 175, this photo shows Hptm. Siebelt Reents with other pilots from the 1.J/88. In the background is Reents' Bf 109 E.

ABOVE: The aircraft to the left of this photograph, coded 6●121, was flown by Oblt. Karl-Wolfgang Redlich of 2.J/88. Redlich later took over command of I./JG 27 in 1944, but was killed on 29 May of that year. He claimed four victories in Spain and was awarded the Ritterkreuz in 1941.

ABOVE: One of the last Bf 109 Es to arrive in Spain, 6●125, was delivered to 1.J/88 but saw little operational service before it was handed over to the Spanish Air Force and the conclusion of the conflict.

LEFT: While mechanics work on a pair of Bf 109 E-3s others scan the sky for other Messerschmitts. The E-series Bf 109 was by far the best fighter to see service in the Spanish Civil War.

The Mickey Mouse emblem was first painted on the He 51 of 3.J/88 piloted by Oblt. Douglas Pitcairn by one of his Staffel's mechanics. The Staffel had christened itself, among other things, "The Deep Sea Divers from the Race of Mickey Mouse", a reference to the sharp diving tactics employed by the unit's aircraft. The emblem was later adopted by the remainder of the Staffel and appeared in several slightly modified forms.

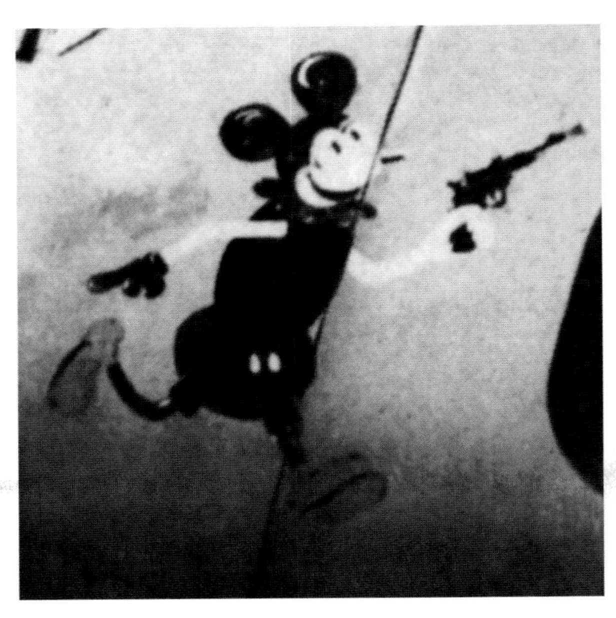

BELOW: Oblt. Hans Schmoller-Haldy's Bf 109 E-3, coded 6●123 showing clearly, the 3.Staffel's Mickey Mouse emblem and Schmoller-Haldy's personal badge depicting an overflowing beer mug.

RIGHT: Oblt. Hans Schmoller-Haldy in his Bf 109 E-3 (see below opposite) in March 1939. This view clearly shows the aircraft 's code 6●123, as well as the Mickey Mouse badge of 3.J/88 and Schmoller-Haldy's personal insignia, an overflowing beer mug was also carried. The initials "CP" were to commemorate the "Order of Cardinal Paff" - an international pilots' drinking club founded in Belgium.

BELOW: Oblt. Hans Schmoller-Haldy (right) of 3.J/88 sitting on the wing of his Bf 109 D-1 at Sanjurjo/Zaragoza. Note the small exhaust ejection stubs that were a feature of the D-series Bf 109.

ABOVE AND LEFT:
The emblems carried on Schmoller-Haldy's Bf 109 E. The "Mickey Mouse" badge was similar to that carried on Werner Mölders' Bf 109 D-1.

Messerschmitt Bf 109 E-3
Flown by Oblt. Hans Schmoller-Haldy of 3.J/88, March 1939. His aircraft carried the Mickey Mouse badge of 3.J/88 which was first painted on Douglas Pitcairn's machine. In addition, his personal insignia, an overflowing beer mug was also applied illustrating his membership of the "Cardinal Paff" drinking club.

ABOVE: This close-up of a Bf 109 E shows the red oil filler triangle positioned behind the carburettor air intake with the inscription "INTAVA" underneath. The pilot has slid back the glass panel in his canopy.

ABOVE: Several units in the Legion Condor had the cartoon character Mickey Mouse painted on their aircraft. This He 111, photographed at Burgos in July 1937, has a variation of the emblem with the legend "Viva Micky" painted below

RIGHT: A mechanic strips off the cowling from the 1,100 hp Daimler-Benz DB 601 A twelve-cylinder inverted Vee liquid cooled engine which powered the Bf 109 E. Above the engine can be seen the two 7.9mm MG 17 machine-guns, each of which carried 1,000 rounds.

LEFT: One of the last Bf 109 E-3s, coded 6●126, photographed at Barcelona's El Prat de Lobregat airfield close to the end of the Spanish Civil War. The spinner of this aircraft was unusual in being painted white. Like most Bf 109s in Spain, this aircraft was later taken over by the new Spanish Air Force.

BELOW: The former Austrian fighter pilot, Lt. Josef "Joschko" Fözö achieved three victories in Spain. This photograph shows his aircraft after he completed a landing at Barcience but forgot to lower his undercarriage! Fözö was later to command II./JG 51 before being seriously injured in a take-off accident.

ABOVE: Being unused to retractable undercarriages pilots often forget to extend the wheels of their Bf 109s before landing! However this aircraft, a Bf 109 D, looks as though it suffered engine failure because the propeller appears undamaged.

BELOW: After the end in Spain, several Bf 109s were assembled at Recajo-Logroño airfield where they were handed over to the new Spanish Air Force (the Ejercito del Aire). The photo shows a variety of variants including a Bf 109 B-2 (coded 6●40), a Bf 109 C-1 (6●47) and a Bf 109 E-3, (6●111).

July 1938-March 1939

ABOVE: Members of the naval reconnaissance squadron AS/88 on their way back to Germany at the end of the war. The words chalked on the side of the train can be translated as: "We want to go home to the Reich"!

RIGHT: The beautiful Spanish certificate awarding the Medalla de la Lampana to "Capitan" Dietrich von Bothmer on 1 December 1938 at Burgos.

VNA GRANDE LIBRE

PLVS VLTRA

Ejército Español

En atención a los méritos contraídos en Operaciones de Guerra por Capitan Dietrich von Bothmer

S. E. el Jefe del Estado y Generalísimo de los Ejércitos Nacionales ha tenido á bien concederle la Medalla de la Campaña

Y para que conste y para satisfacción del interesado, expido en nombre de S. E. el presente diploma en Burgos a 1.° de Diciembre de 1938, III Año Triunfal.

El Ministro de Defensa Nacional

Fidel Dávila

MINISTERIO DE DEFENSA NACIONAL

CENTRE LEFT: Probably the last but one Bf 109 sent to Spain was coded 6●130. It was an E-3 model with two 20 mm MG FF cannon in the wings.

LEFT: It has been thought that only 130 Bf 109s were sent to Spain, but this photograph seems to prove that at least one more machine arrived with the code 6●131. The pilot in the foreground is Gerhard Halupczek (later Herzog). This photo also shows to advantage the black patch painted around the exhaust area of many Bf 109s in Spain.

BELOW: At the end of the Spanish Civil War many of the surviving aircraft were either dismantled or taken over by the Spanish Airforce. Here Bf 109s are being dismantled and crated ready for transport. Note the code of the aircraft in the front centre has been overpainted in black and the wings and tail surfaces have been removed.

MARCH TO MAY 1939

Return in Triumph

Following the Nationalist victory, celebratory parades were organised throughout April and May 1939 by the Legion Condor in Sevilla, Valencia, Barajas, Madrid and León. After this, J/88's Bf 109s were handed over to the Spanish, some remaining in service with that air force for many years. As for the German pilots, many of them were to become famous during a war which was to surpass even that in Spain for its ferocity and destruction.

On 28 May, the entire Legion Condor left the port of Vigo by ship for Hamburg. Here they were met by *Generalfeldmarschall* Hermann Göring who informed them that they would be assembled at Berlin-Döberitz for a grand parade in front of the *Führer.* The parade, comprising 14,000 men took place on 6 June 1939, when the Legion was finally dissolved. As the airmen discarded their brown Legion Condor uniforms for the more familiar blue of the *Luftwaffe*, that force possessed fifteen single-engined fighter units equipped with the various versions of the Bf 109 including the new E. These, their bases and commanders were:

I.(leicht J)/LG 2	Garz	*Major* Hanns Trübenbach
I./JG 130	Jesau	*Hptm.* Bernhard Woldenga
I./JG 131 *"Richthofen"*	Döberitz	*Major* Carl Viek
I./JG 132 *"Schlageter"*	Köln	*Major* Gotthard Handrick
II./JG 132 *"Schlageter"*	Düsseldorf	*Hptm.* Werner Palm
I./JG 133	Wiesbaden	*Major* Hans-Hugo Witt
II./JG 133	Mannheim	*Major* Hubertus Merhardt von Bernegg
I./JG 134	Wien (Vienna)	*Hptm.* Wilfried Müller-Rienzburg
I./JG 231	Bernburg	*Hptm.* Hannes Gentzen
II./JG 231	Zerbst	*Major* Wolf-Heinrich von Houwald
I./JG 233	Bad Aibling	*Major* Max Ibel
I./JG 331	Mährisch–Trübau	*Obstlt.* Theo Osterkamp
I./JG 333	Herzogenaurach	*Major* Stoltenhoff
II./JG 333	Marienbad	*Major* Carl Schumacher
I./JG 433	Böblingen	*Hptm.* Dietrich von Pfeil und Klein Ellguth

In addition, there were eight *Zerstörer* or destroyer wings available. These were in the process of exchanging their Bf 109s for the new twin-engine Bf 110. These units were I. and II./JG 141 (formed from II. and III./JG 132), I., II. and III./JG 142 (formed from I., II. and IV./JG 134), I./JG 143 (formed from III./JG 234) and I./JG 144 (formed from III./JG 334) plus the II.*(schwere J) Gruppe* of the *Lehrgeschwader.*

On 1 December 1938, a special *Trägerjagdstaffel* (carrier fighter squadron) had been formed to operate Bf 109s from the aircraft carrier *Graf Zeppelin* which was launched a week later. This unit, 6.(J)/186, was formed at Kiel-Holtenau under *Hptm.* Heinrich Seeliger. Training was carried out using an artificial landing strip with the same dimensions as that planned for the carrier.

On 19 May 1939, a large parade was held in Madrid to celebrate the victory of the Nationalists. As part of the aerial display, a group of German, Italian and Spanish pilots flew over the crowd with their aircraft in formation spelling out the name "FRANCO".

To celebrate the Nationalist victory in Spain, a huge parade was held in Madrid on 12 May 1939. As part of the aerial display a group of Spanish aircraft flew in formation imitating the Falange, the symbol of the Nationalists.

March to May 1939

LEFT: Oblt. Helmut-Felix Bolz of 3./J88 poses in front of a captured Polikarpov I-16 "Rata" at a parade held after the end of the war at Sanjurjo/Zaragoza.
For this parade, ten I-16s were ferried to Sanjurjo/Zaragoza airfield.

RIGHT: Oblt. Hans Schmoller-Haldy standing in front of a Polikarpov I-15 "Chato" (often known as a "Curtiss") coded CA-030 belonging to the 2nd Squadron of Group 26 which arrived in Barajas on 30 March 1936. This photo was taken after the end of the Spanish Civil War.

BELOW: A line-up of Nationalist aircraft taken during one of the victory parades held at Sevilla on 17 April, at Valencia on 3 May, at Barajas on 12 May, at Madrid on 19 May and at León on 22 May. Second from the right is the former Legion Condor Bf 109 D-1, coded 6●56, which was previously flown by Handrick and Grabmann, and, far right, a He 112. The Bf 109 was later taken over by the Spanish 1a Ea of the Grupo 5-G-5. Codes 6●51 to 6●86 were allocated to Bf 109 D-1s sent to Spain.

BELOW: The city of León pays homage to the Legion Condor.

ABOVE: "Hauptfeldwebel" Hans Seliger (left) leading a group of men from 3.J/88 as they leave León to return to Germany in May 1939. Taken just before boarding the boat for Germany at Abmarsch near León. The Hauptfeldwebel, or "Spiess" as he was colloquially called, was the NCO administrative head of a company or corresponding unit (Staffel, battery etc.). His rank could be anything from an Unteroffizier to a Stabsfeldwebel. Seliger later acted as "Spiess" in JG 54.

LEFT: A group of pilots from 3.J/88 at Vigo, waiting for the boat to Germany. On the left is Lt. Kurt Sochatzky (with cigarette), a future holder of the Ritterkreuz, who came at the campaign's end and Oblt. Hans Schmoller-Haldy, is third from left.

Commanders of the "Legion Condor " Jagdgruppe 88

3 November 1936 to 28 March 1939

"Legion Condor"

From	To	Commander
3 Nov 36	30 Oct 37	*Gen.Maj.* Hugo Sperrle
30 Oct 37	1 Dec 38	*Gen.Maj.* Hellmuth Volkmann
1 Dec 38	28 Mar 39	*Gen.Maj.* Wolfram *Freiherr* von Richthofen

Jagdgruppe 88

From	To	Commander
3 Nov 36	18 July 37	*Major* Hubertus Merhardt von Bernegg
18 Jul 37	10 Sep 38	*Hptm.* Gotthard Handrick
10 Sep 38	28 Mar 39	*Hptm.* Walter Grabmann[1]

1. Staffel

From	To	Commander
3 Nov 36	6 Apr 37	*Hptm.* Werner Palm
6 Apr 37	18 Dec 37	*Hptm.* Harro Harder
19 Dec 37	2 Sep 38	*Hptm.* Wolfgang Schellmann
2 Sep 38	28 Mar 39	*Hptm.* Siebelt Reents

2. Staffel

From	To	Commander
3 Nov 36	6 Apr 37	*Oblt.* Otto Lehmann
19 Mar 37	6 Sep 37	*Oblt.* Günther Lützow
6 Sep 37	28 May 38	*Oblt.* Joachim Schlichting
28 May 38	31 Oct 38	*Oblt.* Hubert Kroeck
1 Nov 38	28 Mar 39	*Oblt.* Alfred von Lojewski

3. Staffel

From	To	Commander
3 Nov 36	Apr 37	*Oblt.* Jürgen Roth
Apr 37	26 Jul 37	*Oblt.* Douglas Pitcairn
27 Jul 37	24 May 38	*Oblt.* Adolf Galland
24 May 38	5 Dec 38	*Oblt.* Werner Mölders
5 Dec 38	28 Mar 39	*Oblt.* Hubertus von Bonin

4. Staffel

(The designation of the original He 51 unit after the arrival of the Legion Condor, the original 4. Staffel of J/88 was disbanded in March 1937)

From	To	Commander
6 Aug 38	13 Nov 36	*Oblt.* Kraft Eberhardt
13 Nov 36	1 Mar 37	*Hptm.* Herwig Knüppel
1 Mar 37	Mar 37	*Oblt.* Walter Kienzle

(A new 4.J/88 was formed on 2 November 1937 and disbanded on 17 June 1938)

From	To	Commander
2 Nov 37	17 Jun 38	*Oblt.* Eberhard von Trützschler-d'Élsa

5. Staffel

(For a short time, from 15 February 1938, the Jolanthe Stukakette equipped with the Ju 87 was redesignated 5.J/88).

1. Hptm. Hans-Heinrich Brustellin was planned to succeed Grabmann, but the war came to an end before this appointment came into effect.

March to May 1939

RIGHT: Hitler takes the salute at the massive parade held in Berlin on 6 June 1939 to honour the 14,000 men of the Legion Condor who served in Spain.

ABOVE: "Memories of our time in Spain 1937-38".

RIGHT: Göring (centre) salutes the men of the Legion Condor after their return to Germany. At his side is Generalmajor Wolfram Freiherr von Richthofen, a cousin of the famous ace of the First World War. After the Legion Condor was disbanded, von Richthofen took over the VIII. Fliegerkorps, then Luftflotte 4 and finally Luftflotte 2. He contracted a brain tumour in November 1944 and died in July 1945.

RIGHT: The last commander of the Legion Condor, Generalmajor Wolfram Freiherr von Richthofen, greets Göring on his return to Germany. At the left of the picture, behind von Richthofen, is Oberst Alexander von Scheele who established the Reisegesellschaft (Tourist Company) which transported volunteers to Spain. Von Scheele later became military head of HISMA.

Im Namen
des
Deutschen Volkes
verleihe ich

dem Oberleutnant Dietrich v. Bothmer

in Anerkennung
seiner hervorragenden Leistungen
als Freiwilliger im spanischen Freiheitskampf
das
Deutsche Spanien-Kreuz
in
Gold mit Schwertern

Berlin, den 6. Juni 1939.

Der Führer
und
Oberste Befehlshaber
der Wehrmacht

RIGHT: The German certificate awarding the Deutsche Spanien-Kreuz in Gold mit Schwerten (German Spanish Gold Cross with Swords) on 6 June 1939 to Oblt. Dietrich von Bothmer.

ABOVE: During the parade held in Berlin before Hitler on 6 June 1939 to honour the men of the Legion Condor, 330 members of the Hitler Youth held banners each commemorating an individual who fell in the conflict. This tribute was installed in front of the Technical University.

RIGHT: This monument was built to remember the fighter pilots who lost their lives while serving with the Legion Condor. Those recorded were: Oblt. Kraft Eberhardt killed in combat on 13 November 1936 while commanding 4.J/88, Lt. Oskar Henrici killed in combat on the same day, Lt. Hans Peter von Gallera killed in combat on 6 January 1937 in the Madrid area, Uffz. Kurt Kneiding, killed in the same combat; Uffz. Emil Rückert, killed on 25 March 1937 by anti-aircraft fire; Uffz. Guido Höness, killed in combat on 13 July 1937 and Lt. Ernst Reutter, killed on 24 April 1937, shot down by Flak.

BELOW: Spanish personnel loading the remains of a crashed Bf 109 on to a truck in Catalonia. It is interesting to note that all markings have been painted out.

LEFT: These two Bf 109s, coded 23●15 (a B-1) and 23●3 (a B-2) were photographed several years after the war in Spain on Banolas airfield. Their duty was to intercept French transport aircraft en route for Algeria which might have violated Spanish airspace. The aircraft, belonging to the 23rd Fighter Regiment, carry the red-yellow-red roundels of the post-war Spanish Air Force. Note the code C4-... just in front of the tail. Unfortunately it is impossible to read the number that follows, because it would have been the same as that used by the Legion Condor.

Detail of the badge painted on the fin of the Spanish He 112s

ABOVE: A Spanish Heinkel He 112 B-0 fighter in the markings of Grupo 27 photographed in February 1940. A total of sixteen He 112s, coded 5●52 to 5●67, were delivered to the Spanish Air Force, only two aircraft serving with the Legion Condor.

RIGHT: Illustrated in colour below this aircraft crashed landed at Melilla in Spanish Morocco in 1942.

Heinkel He 112 B-0

Operated by Grupo 27 of the Spanish Air Force. One of the last He 112s delivered to Spain, this aircraft crash landed in August 1942 at Melilla in Spanish Morocco. The drawing indicates how Spanish Air Force markings evolved after the Civil War ended, the black circles with white crosses on the wings being replaced by a red, yellow and red roundel. The camouflage was similar to that carried by German operated aircraft of the late 1930s.

Was I a coward? No, I don't think so, I simply panicked.

HANS SCHMOLLER-HALDY

Oblt. Hans Schmoller-Haldy was *Gruppenadjudant* of I./JG 135 and later served with 3.J/88."After serving for three months in Austria following the *"Anschluss"*, I returned to Bad Aibling, my home base, in order to see if all was well there. I was later joined by the *Kommandeur* and the *Staffelkapitäne* because there was little military activity in Wien (Vienna) at that time.

As the *Gruppenadjudant*, I had to prepare a daily list of effective pilots, at the head which I was told to put the names of four or five unmarried pilots with high skill who would volunteer for special missions. In fact, we all knew that German pilots were involved in Spain and several pilots came to me asking to be sent to the Legion. Paradoxically, if somebody had said publicly that we were involved in Spain, he would have been immediately sent to a concentration camp.

When the Legion Condor needed new pilots, my *Kommandeur,* Max Ibel, would receive a coded telegram, known only to me and my commander, from the *RLM* (German Aviation Ministry), which always read: *"JG 135 meldet umgehend X Flugzeugführer für Sonderstab W"* (JG 135 immediately reports X number of pilots to Sonderstab W"). I would then give Ibel the pilot's list, kept in a safe and he would chose those who would be sent. Of course, I had wanted to put my name amongst those at the top in the hope of going to Spain, but Ibel said he needed me because the *Gruppenadjudant* was his replacement when he was away, which occurred quite often.

One Saturday evening at the end of November 1938, I received orders to be in Berlin on Monday by late afternoon. Next day, a Sunday, my family (both parents, my brother and sister) had planned a midday meal. I did not say a word about my departure due to strict security restrictions. At the meal's end, I said goodbye to everyone, my father accompanied me to my car and asked, putting his hands on my shoulders: "What's the matter? Why are you so silent?". I took his hands away and quickly climbed into the car to hide my emotions. I just said: "Nothing, I'm just the same as I always am". I drove away. The only person I told was my closest friend, "Pips" Priller (later to become a well known ace) to whom I entrusted several of my personal belongings including my car and uniform. A few days after my departure, my family received a telegram from the *RLM* explaining that I had been sent on a special mission and that they should not talk about my absence to anyone. They were also given a private address in Berlin where they could write, however, no official service was ever mentioned.

When I arrived in Berlin, I went to the given address where I spent the night. At about six o'clock the next morning I was driven in a plain car to Staaken where I met about 15 other men dressed in civilian clothes like me. Amongst them, I recognised several pilots who I had met previously at training schools or at the Richthofen *Geschwader*. Shortly afterwards, we were flown in a Ju 52 from Berlin to Italy. The aircraft was fitted with special auxiliary tanks to extend its endurance to at least eight hours and also carried a second crew. Perhaps because of the miserable weather, we landed first at Milan before going on to Rome. Next day we transferred to Spain, landing at the La Cenia base where we were welcomed by a German in a Spanish uniform. I reported to my new *Kommandeur*, Major Grabmann who sent me to the third *Staffel* under *Oblt.* von Bonin. I liked him immediately; he was a good pilot and an excellent officer. His aristocratic origins were easy to guess.

After a few days, von Bonin told me that I was to fly my first combat mission. This was during the last days of 1938. Our Technical Officer, *Oblt.* Bolz, gave me the Bf 109 formerly piloted by Mölders which was probably to give me confidence.

After take off we quickly attained 4,000 m (13,000 ft) and headed for Barcelona. I think I was the first (there were six of us flying the mission) to sight a group of Ratas. I always had very good eyesight which probably saved my life many times during my long fighter career. I waggled my wings to warn my *Rottenführer* (*Oblt.* Bolz). About six to seven minutes later they were on us. No aerial combat followed, just total confusion. For my part, I tried to avoid fighting, hoping that I wouldn't be shot down. I climbed at full power. It was probably the first time that Mölders' aircraft had performed such a manoeuvre. Was I a coward? No, I don't think so, I simply panicked. I just found myself alone in a dangerous situation, flying over a strange landscape in a foreign country. Fortunately, I had fairly good directional sense and did not need to recognise the landscape. I returned to where we had started fighting, and my intuition gave me the correct course home. With surprising certainty, I flew in the right direction. I soon found the church which I had sighted just after take-off and considered a good landmark. I now knew that within nine minutes I would be over the base. In the meantime, bad weather had moved in over the airfield, almost hiding the ground. In spite of the terrible conditions, I was the first to return and managed to land without difficulty before surprised eyes! In total, I flew 68 missions in Spain. I achieved no victories but was not shot down either. However, I did have to make one emergency landing due to an engine failure.

I also took part in the big parades held in Spain during April and May 1939 and was amongst the last contingent, officers and men, to leave. Our *Jagdgruppe* was amongst the last to embark at Vigo for Hamburg. Our unit was a reinforced group – about 700 men instead of the normal strength of 500. Each *Staffel* had about 16 pilots instead the normal twelve in Germany. Shortly before we embarked for Germany we were asked: "Who would you like to see first on your arrival in Berlin?" I replied: "My father". Consequently, he was there when we had our huge parade on 6th June 1939.

A day or so before this parade, we were instructed in the Döberitz area on how to get to the centre of Berlin. On the 6th, at about 05.00 hours, our contingent of about 5,000 soldiers were already in place for the march. South Berlin was sealed off so that no cars could enter. We were ordered to reach our departure position at a certain time with our unit at the head of the column. We started off in the direction of the *Brandenburger Tor* (Brandenburg Gate), and after about 1,500 metres, we arrived at a massive square where we took up our positions. The square was full of young boys and girls from the *Hitler Jugend*, and thousands of cheering people. We began to march, parading past several stands full of NSDAP officials and eventually before Hitler in uniform.

After the parade, we received a message from the *Führer.* He wrote: "I am so proud of you all," and invited the *Kommandeure* and *Staffelkapitäne* to his *Reichs Chancellery*. As this did not concern me, I returned to the airfield, put on my civilian clothes and went home. I had received three weeks leave and was also pleased to see that my bank balance had swollen to over 7,000 *Reichsmarks*. With this time and money, I flew to North Africa.

I finally returned to Germany shortly before the war began without any idea of how the political situation had developed. Not one of us would have imagined that a war in Western Europe was so close."

Prelude to Poland 1939

The experience gained by German pilots in Spain was to prove invaluable when the Second World War broke out. For the fighter units, perhaps the most important operational lesson learned was the improvement of tactics. Like most other air forces they began the war in Spain by flying in tight parade ground groups of three, but by the end they had adopted a looser more manoeuvrable formation of four, known as the *Schwarm.* In addition to gaining operational experience, many pilots brought back with them their unit or personal emblems, applying these to their *Luftwaffe* Bf 109s.

The next major operation in which the *Jagdwaffe* became involved was the invasion of Bohemia and Moravia on 15 March 1939. A total of 500 *Luftwaffe* aircraft took part in the action, with paratroops landing in Prague. This event, and the ceding of the Lithuanian port of Memel to Germany, increased the likelihood of war developing against Germany by Britain and France. The *Luftwaffe* was thus placed on a war footing with a full scale reorganisation of its operational units. This rearrangement is discussed in detail in "BLITZKRIEG ON POLAND".

Messerschmitt Bf 109 E-1
Flown by Ofw. Heinz Bär of 1./JG 51, summer 1939. Many of the unit emblems adopted in Spain were transferred to German units as pilots returned to the mother country. The "Mickey Mouse" badge, which was first painted on Oblt. Douglas Pitcairn's He 51, was later adopted by 1./JG 233 (which later became 1./JG 51). Pitcairn was the unit's Staffelkapitän.

LEFT: When Douglas Pitcairn took over command of 1./JG 51 (formerly 1./JG 233) he retained the Mickey Mouse badge which one of his mechanics had introduced on his aircraft in Spain to indentify his unit. This Bf 109 E was flown by Fw. Heinz Bär who was eventually to command JG 3 and, finally, JV 44. Like most of his subsequent aircraft, including his Me 262, Bär's Bf 109 carried the number "13"

Prelude to Poland 1939

Messerschmitt Bf 109 E-1

In April 1939, JG 132 "Schlageter" was one of the first Luftwaffe units to re-equip with the Bf 109 E. This aircraft, from the 6. Staffel, had black-green (70) and dark green (71) uppersurfaces with pale blue (65) beneath. The "script S" badge of the Geschwader was to become famous during the Battle of Britain period by which time the unit had been redesignated as the famous JG 26.

The badge of JG 132 (later JG 26) "Schlageter", as carried in April 1939

The "Steinbock" (Ram) badge, was used first by 6./JG 132 and later by 6./JG 26 until September 1940. It appeared in various colours including white, brown and silver.

ABOVE: Illustrated in colour above, this Bf 109 E-1 was delivered to 6./JG 132 which became 6./JG 26 in May 1939. The number "12" was painted in bright yellow outlined in black. This photo shows to advantage the fuel filler point between the "2" and the fuselage Balkenkreuz. This was marked by a yellow triangle edged in white with the number "87" indicating the octane rating of the fuel added in black.

LEFT: Another early Bf 109 E-1 of 6./JG 132 coded "Yellow 14"

Prelude to Poland 1939

ABOVE: This Bf 109 E-1 was operated by 1./JG 331, a unit formed from 10./JG 132 "Richthofen" in November 1938. IV./JG 132, of which the 10.Staffel was a part, carried a small coloured circle aft of the fuselage Balkenkreuz to identify that Gruppe. The battered boot badge of I./JG 331 (later I./JG 77) represented "Wanderzirkus Janke" (Jahnke's travelling circus), after the unit's first commander, Hptm. Johannes Janke.

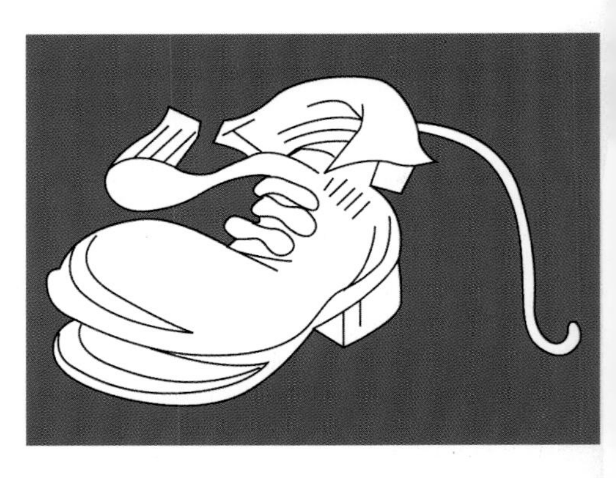

Originally the battered boot badge of I./JG 331 (nick-named "Wanderzirkus Janke") was retained when the unit was redesignated I./JG 77 in May 1939

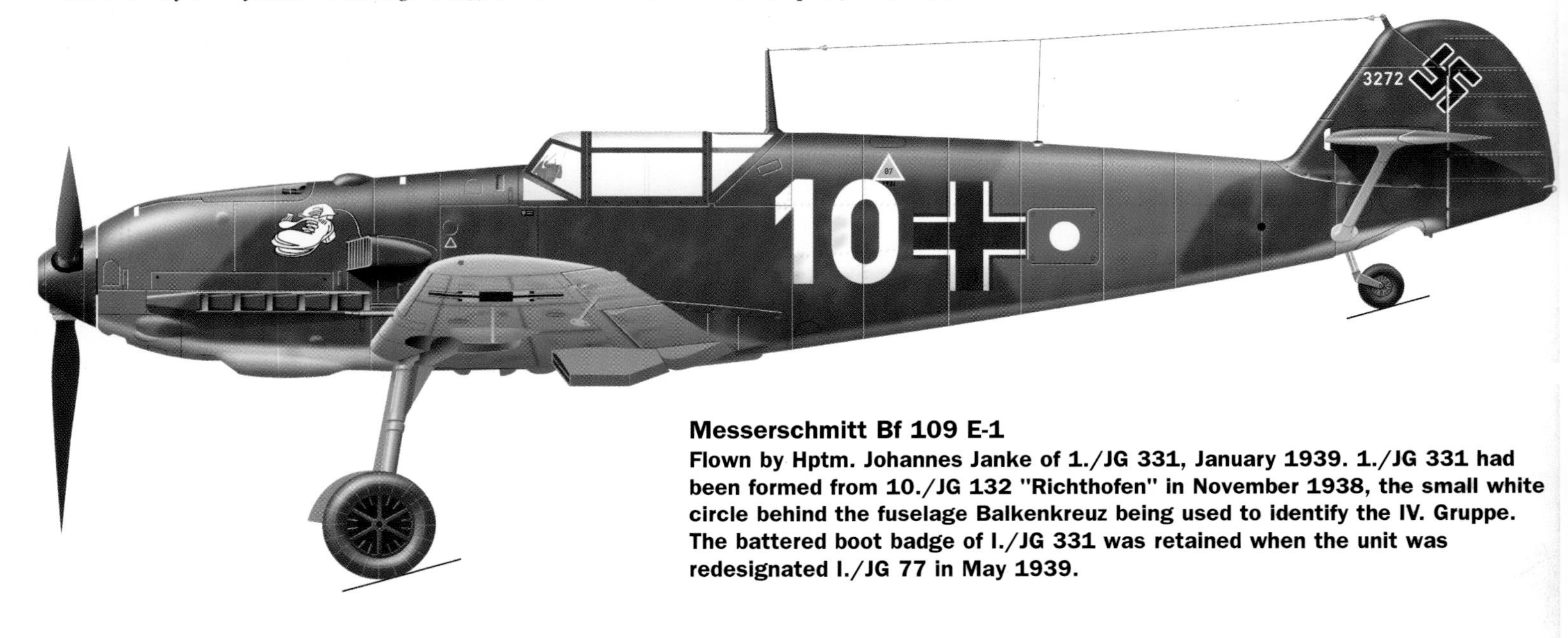

Messerschmitt Bf 109 E-1

Flown by Hptm. Johannes Janke of 1./JG 331, January 1939. 1./JG 331 had been formed from 10./JG 132 "Richthofen" in November 1938, the small white circle behind the fuselage Balkenkreuz being used to identify the IV. Gruppe. The battered boot badge of I./JG 331 was retained when the unit was redesignated I./JG 77 in May 1939.

The Träger-Gruppe 186 adopted the "Graf Zeppelin" family crest as its unit emblem. The only German aircraft carrier, named "Graf Zeppelin", was launched on 8 December 1938.

BELOW: A special Trägerjagdstaffel (carrier fighter squadron) was formed on 1 December 1938 designated 6.(J)/186. It was established to fly Bf 109s from the aircraft carrier Graf Zeppelin which was launched on 8 December 1938. This photograph shows one of the unit's Bf 109 B-2s at Kiel-Holtenau showing the "Graf Zeppelin" family crest painted on the fuselage used as the unit emblem.